Workbook

for use with

News Writing and Reporting for Today's Media

Sixth Edition

Bruce D. Itule
Arizona State University

Douglas A. Anderson
The Pennsylvania State University

Prepared by
Janet Soper
Arizona State University

Boston, Massachusetts   Burr Ridge, Illinois
Dubuque, Iowa   Madison, Wisconsin   New York, New York
San Francisco, California   St. Louis, Missouri

Workbook for use with
NEWS WRITING AND REPORTING FOR TODAY'S MEDIA
Bruce D. Itule, Douglas A. Anderson

Published by McGraw-Hill, an imprint of The McGraw-Hill Companies, Inc., 1221 Avenue of the Americas, New York, NY 10020.

2 3 4 5 6 7 8 9 BKM BKM 0 9 8 7 6 5 4 3

ISBN 0-07-249214-7

www.mhhe.com

The McGraw-Hill Companies

Contents

To the Instructor v

To the Student vi

Part One The Fourth Estate

Chapter 1 Today's Media 3

Chapter 2 Ingredients of News 7

Part Two The Rudiments

Chapter 3 Qualities of Good Writing 13

Chapter 4 Summary Leads 21

Chapter 5 Special Leads 33

Chapter 6 Organizing a News Story 41

Chapter 7 Developing a News Story 47

Chapter 8 Quotations and Attribution 50

Chapter 9 Features 59

Part Three Gathering Information

Chapter 10 Interviewing 67

Chapter 11 Computer-Assisted Reporting and Research 74

Chapter 12 Surveys 81

Part Four Basic Assignments

Chapter 13 Obituaries 93

Chapter 14 News Releases 103

Chapter 15 Speeches and Press Conferences 109

Chapter 16 Weather and Disasters 122

Chapter 17 Broadcast Writing 132

Part Five Beats

Chapter 18 Multicultural Reporting 141

Chapter 19 City Government 146

Chapter 20 Police and Fire 158

Chapter 21 Courts 169

Chapter 22 Sports 195

Part Six Advanced Assignments

Chapter 23 In-depth and Investigative Reporting 205

Chapter 24 Business News and Other Specialties 210

Part Seven Beyond the Writing

Chapter 25 Law 219

Chapter 26 Ethics and Fairness: Responsibility to Society 226

Permissions and Credits 237

To the Instructor

We wrote this workbook to acccompany the sixth edition of *News Writing and Reporting for Today's Media.* The purposes of the workbook are to reinforce the instructional principles outlined in the text and to bridge the gap between theory and practice by providing students with realistic, challenging exercises.

Each chapter of the workbook is based on the corresponding chapter of the textbook, and most consist of two sections: first, a series of Review Questions; and, following them, Suggested Exercises.

To the greatest extent possible, the exercises are based on real news events. "Springdale, U.S.A." exercises tend to bore students. Therefore, we have devised exercises to stimulate students by making them feel that they are at a reporter's desk in a newsroom rather than at a student's desk in a classroom. For example, students will be writing stories based on information that was used to write a weather story for *The Beaumont* (Texas) *Enterprise;* an earthquake story for The Associated Press; a city council story for the *Colorado Springs* (Colo.) *Gazette Telegraph;* and a personality profile for the business section of *The Daily Herald* in Arlington Heights, Ill.

We have also written an instructor's manual that provides answers to all the review questions as well as instructional suggestions from us and from professional journalists. Whenever a workbook exercise is based on an actual story, we reprint that story in the instructor's manual so that your students can compare their stories with those that were printed. In other cases we give you our suggestions on how we thought the lead or story could have been written.

This workbook contains more exercises than students would actually be expected to complete. By offering several possibilities, we are giving instructors the chance to select those that will best serve their students' needs.

We think that this workbook is a convenient, logically organized supplement to *News Writing and Reporting for Today's Media.*

Bruce D. Itule

Douglas A. Anderson

To the Student

As we note in our message to your instructor on page v, the purposes of this workbook are to reinforce the instructional principles outlined in the text and to bridge the gap between theory and practice by providing you with realistic, challenging exercises.

Naturally, your instructor will make specific workbook assignments. Keep in mind, though, that your use of the workbook need not be limited to assignments from your instructor. For example, your instructor may or may not require you to answer the review questions at the beginning of each chapter, orally or in writing as a formal assignment. If you are not required to answer them, you may want to anyway. If you can answer the review questions, you can be assured that you have a good grasp of the material in the corresponding chapter in the textbook.

There are more exercises in the workbook than your instructor would ever assign. That does not mean, however, that you cannot work on exercises at your discretion, particularly in those chapters where you are not confident of your level of expertise.

This workbook is very much a *supplement* to the textbook. Use it to your best advantage.

Bruce D. Itule

Douglas A. Anderson

Part One

The Fourth Estate

1

Today's Media

Review Questions

1 What are the four basic functions writers for any medium must be able to perform?

2 What is the Internet? How would you find today's top story in the largest newspaper in your state?

3 Discuss the three general forms of reporting.

4 Discuss what the following people do in a newspaper newsroom.

a Managing editor

b News editor

c Copy editor

d City editor

e State editor

f National editor

g Photo editor

h Graphics editor

i Sports editor

j Lifestyle editor

k Financial editor

5 Explain the differences between a morning (A.M.) and an evening (P.M.) newspaper.

6 There is a two-car crash at the busiest intersection in town, and two people are killed. There are more accidents at this intersection than at any other in town. The accident occurs during the morning rush hour. How would a reporter working on the P.M. cycle cover this story? How about a reporter for the A.M. cycle?

7 What later stories on the two-car crash could a beat reporter write? How about a specialty reporter?

2

Ingredients of News

Review Questions

1 Define *news.*

2 Define and give examples of hard news events.

3 Define and give examples of soft news events.

4 Define *convergence.* Give an example of convergence in coverage of a national or local story.

5 What is *civic journalism?*

6 Who are the news media gatekeepers, and what do they do?

7 List and discuss the six criteria that are most often considered to determine newsworthiness.

8 In addition to the criteria that editors most often consider to determine newsworthiness, the chapter discusses factors that influence whether a story is published. List and discuss these factors.

9 Discuss "the wall" between editorial and advertising and how it is changing.

10 When trying to sell stories to an editor, what steps can you follow to increase the possibility that your idea will be accepted?

Suggested Exercises

1 From a daily in your area, clip stories that were published primarily because of their timeliness. Do the same for stories that were published primarily because of proximity, conflict, eminence and prominence, consequence and impact, and human interest. Would any of the stories have been selected because they met more than one of the criteria?

2 Compare the front pages of a metropolitan daily and a small-circulation daily from your area. What are the similarities? What are the differences? For example, what stories are covered? Where are the stories placed on the page? How much art is used? Which newspaper uses more wire stories?

3 List the front-page stories from the metropolitan daily. Determine if the stories were selected on the basis of the traditional news elements, such as timeliness, proximity and so forth. What other factors did the editors and reporters likely consider in making story decisions?

4 List the front-page stories from the small-circulation daily. Determine if the stories were selected on the basis of the traditional news elements, such as timeliness, proximity and so forth. What other factors did the editors and reporters likely consider in making story decisions?

5 Examine both the metropolitan daily and the small-circulation newspaper to determine the news mix. How many stories would be categorized as hard news? How many would be categorized as soft news?

6 Monitor a local or cable midday television newscast. List all the stories broadcast and the approximate time devoted to each. Compare the stories featured on the newscast with those in an area newspaper for that day. What are the differences? What are the similarities? Do you see any evidence of convergence?

Part Two

The Rudiments

3

Qualities of Good Writing

Review Questions

1 The text reprints a portion of Roy Peter Clark's *Washington Journalism Review* article in which he discusses 14 common traits of good writers. List and discuss these traits.

a Trait 1

b Trait 2

c Trait 3

d Trait 4

e Trait 5

f Trait 6

g Trait 7

h Trait 8

i Trait 9

j Trait 10

k Trait 11

l Trait 12

m Trait 13

n Trait 14

2 The text lists Robert Gunning's "Ten Principles of Clear Writing." List and discuss these principles.

a Principle 1

b Principle 2

c Principle 3

d Principle 4

e Principle 5

f Principle 6

g Principle 7

h Principle 8

i Principle 9

j Principle 10

Suggested Exercises

1 Clip examples from newspapers and magazines to illustrate each of Robert Gunning's 10 principles.

2 Good writing encompasses more than just choosing the right word or phrase. Proper usage, correct spelling and consistent style are also essential. Correct usage, spelling, style and writing errors in the following sentences, referring to the AP style rules in Appendix B of the text when appropriate.

a Things will always turn out okay if people accept one another.

b Aid to Women, an abortion alternative center since January, 1986, focuses their concern on women who are or think they might be pregnant.

c Dunn said to think in terms of the inconvenience the loss of certain items would cause.

d "They assume its a safe environment and don't stop to think," he said.

e Apathy is the number one reason for the backpack thefts on campus, according to the security officer.

f He said many students are packpack theives because of financial problems.

g Mandino is negotiating with other restuarants.

h Boersma, a veteran of three semesters, said "We also do exit interviews for students leaving the school."

i Boersma describes his duties as "making college life a little easier."

j The City Council discussed two proposals that would effect the now-vacant Indian Bend Wash.

k Duncan said he doesn't believe students are willing to spend the money for the lock just to save their belongings.

l Bickey has worked for Southwest Valet for a year and is now Mandino's assistant.

m Employees make between four and six dollars an hour, but the pay will go up beginning around November.

n The clinic is open from 10:30–3:00 Monday, Wednesday, and Thursday.

o The next meeting will be at 3:15 p.m. Wednesday, Sept. 25.

p He said he has been politically active since the 1960's.

q Sam Lane, an aircraft noise consultant from Costa Mesa, California, discussed the proposal.

r Each team was accompanied by two fraternity members acting as coaches.

s The organization has approximately 500,000 active members and over 5 million alumni nationwide.

t Jones said small padlocks for the zipper pulls would prevent thefts which occur while students are in class.

u Mooney aims to educate and inform women about such misconceptions.

v The average age of the women that come to the group is 23.

w Farrell ended by saying, "It is up to all of us to make the choice."

x Due to the lack of student response, Gwinner no longer calls his answering machine a hotline.

y The second part of the campaign is putting educational advertisements in magazines and newspapers.

z Jones said we have no choice but to work with him.

3 Here is the first two-thirds of a story by Alan Greenberg of *The Hartford* (Conn.) *Courant.* Label passages in the story that conform to Gunning's principles. For example: Put action into your verbs ("And he *whipped* himself to the edge of exhaustion doing it, and the sellout crowd into an almost interminable state of ear-splitting frenzy").

BOSTON—Larry Bird's scariest move of the day was his 60-foot walk from dressing room to interview room through the cramped catacombs of Boston Garden. To escort their city's priceless treasure through a grabbing gauntlet of 40 half-crazed, half-drunk, half-naked male fans, the Garden sent two blue-shirted security guards who couldn't have combed Jerry Sichting's hair without a ladder.

It was like shipping the Hope Diamond in a single-ply shopping bag. But Bird, his brand-new green world champions T-shirt already black from post-game sweat and champagne, walked on. As he did, the mob moved in, and the sloping shoulders and broad back that had just carried the Celtics to their 16th National Basketball Association championship were slapped so hard and so often it sounded like hail hitting a tired tin roof.

"You wouldn't believe how bad it hurts to play 42 or 43 minutes and have people slap you on the back," Bird said.

If he and the Celtics had lost Sunday, it would have hurt a lot more. They didn't lose for a lot of reasons. But mostly, they didn't lose because Larry Bird wouldn't let them.

Coming off the Game 5 calamity in Houston, Bird had said it would be this way. He said the Celtics were going to run and rebound in Game 6 with a verve that had virtually vanished on their tiring trip to Texas. And he promised he would lead them. And when Larry Bird gives his word, just be glad you're not the one being sentenced.

To a career already crammed full of finest hours, Larry Bird added another two-hour documentary detailing why he is the greatest basketball player the world has ever seen. He did what he wanted to do on the steamy Garden floor Sunday, which was everything.

And he whipped himself to the edge of exhaustion doing it, and the sellout crowd into an almost interminable state of ear-splitting frenzy. The result was one of the most one-sided runaways in NBA finals history.

But even though the crowd hit its ear-crushing crescendo when a Bird three-pointer and Bill Walton jump shot gave the Celtics an 89-61 lead with 10:20 to go—the final shotgun blast to a tottering team already shot full of holes—Bird refused to take his hand off the trigger until he had 29 points and the Celtics led by 22 with 2:20 left.

Then, and only then, did he feel sufficiently secure to let the delighted Walton lean on him like a 7-foot puppy as they stood there, jiving and high-fiving in front of the Celtics' bench.

Only then, with the crowd calling his name in thanks, with the Rockets reduced to ashes, would he allow the game to go on without him.

"When you're in the game and you've got a 15-to 20-point lead, you don't want someone else to come in and flub it up for you," Bird said. "If we're going to lose the game, I want to be out there."

Until he dropped. Or overwhelmed his opponent.

It didn't take long to see which it was going to be. He made the game's first steal, the first dive for a loose ball. He barged into the Rockets' redwood forest and ripped away rebounds. Some he snared by getting perfect position, others he snatched off the long, higher limbs of Akeem Olajuwon and Ralph Sampson.

"The ball was very wet because of the heat (80 degrees at courtside)," Bird said. "If you got a hand on it, you were going to be able to knock it away."

Unless, of course, you were trying to knock it away from someone named Bird. It was Bird bolting up the court to lead the fast break. Bird barging into the high-flying Olajuwon on a jump ball, then tipping the ball to a disbelieving Dennis Johnson. Bird shooting that silken stepaway jump shot over Rodney McCray. Bird flicking an awesome arrow of a give-and-go pass to the cutting Kevin McHale, only to bite his blond mustache as McHale missed the layup.

At halftime, the Celtics had a 55–38 lead, Bird had eight of their 15 assists, and if McHale hadn't missed more layups Sunday than he'll miss in the next 27 years, he'd have had nearly twice that.

4

Summary Leads

Review Questions

1 What are the two main purposes of a summary lead?

2 Describe the inverted-pyramid form of news writing, and explain why most newspapers use it.

3 What are the five W's and H? Where should they be in a news story?

4 Which W or H is the focal point in each of the following six summary leads?

a The search for a new president for the university has been temporarily postponed.

b Religious displays can continue to be set up in Central Park because there is no law against them, the city attorney said Monday.

c In an effort to increase awareness on campus, the WSU Political Union has appointed a new chairperson, and he plans to use advertising to bring about change.

d Mayor Norman Hendricks announced today that he will not seek re-election next year.

e University Dining Services will attempt to combat the weekly loss of hundreds of dollars by closing the Rotunda and Regents late-night dining areas.

f Sunday has been designated "Quit Smoking and Live Day" throughout the state.

5 What are the factors that can influence how a reporter thinks about a story?

6 What is a multiple-element (or double-barreled) lead? Give an example of one.

7 A summary lead should generally contain no more than how many words?

8 What is a buried lead? Why should it be avoided?

9 What is the preferred position for the time element in a summary lead?

10 What is the active voice? The passive voice? Which is preferred in news writing and why?

11 What is attribution, and why is it needed?

1 Write a summary lead based on the following information, which is from a story by The Associated Press.

A train from Kansas City was headed for Barstow, Calif. The 89-car train was being pulled by four locomotives, and about 27 of the cars were empty.

It was a Burlington Northern Santa Fe Corp. freight train. At least two tankers on the train were carrying hazardous substances. Others carried glass, machinery, heavy equipment, military vehicles, frozen meat, lumber, feed grain, iron and corn syrup.

Sixteen cars of the train derailed early Wednesday morning. The derailment occurred at about 12:15 a.m. It blocked the Santa Fe's two main lines in the Mojave Desert, about 100 miles northeast of Los Angeles. Railroad traffic in and out of Southern California was stopped.

The tracks are also used by Amtrak and Union Pacific railroad.

The train had a crew of two. Neither crew member was hurt.

Neither of the cars carrying hazardous substances was leaking.

Authorities on the scene said they suspected a broken rail was to blame. Mike Martin, a spokesman for Burlington Northern Santa Fe Corp., said the rail break was not considered suspicious.

2 Write a summary lead based on the following information, which is from a story in the *Skokie* (Ill.) *Review.*

A neighbor of a house on Lawler Avenue in Skokie reported a fire just after 7 p.m.

By the time firefighters arrived, flames were shooting out of the windows on the south side of a one-story brick house. The fire was in a bedroom.

Firefighters forced their way into the home because there was no one at home. The owner returned later, when department investigators were on the scene.

Investigators said the fire was caused by a cigarette that apparently was left smoldering on a mattress and pillow.

Skokie Fire Department officials said the fire caused an estimated $50,000 damage. It occurred on Friday night.

3 Write a summary lead based on the following information, which is from a story in the *San Francisco Examiner.*

There has been another winter storm in Northern California.

Snow fell on 4,062-foot Mount Hamilton east of San Jose. It even snowed in Oakland at about 2 a.m. There was snow on Coast Range mountains north and south of San Francisco.

This latest storm occurred on Thursday morning.

It left behind icy roads and frigid temperatures.

There was also some good news. For a change, there's a promise of a dry and sunny day on Friday.

The storm brought snow, hail, torrential rains and standing water on roadways, which caused hundreds of fender-bender accidents in the state.

Rain on already-saturated hillsides created an extreme danger of mudslides, officials said.

4 Write a summary lead based on the following information, which is from a story by The Associated Press.

The Tucson Toros are a minor-league baseball team playing in the Arizona city.

The team general manager is Mike Feder. He was upset on Thursday because a red equipment bag was stolen.

The equipment bag contained the uniform worn by the team's mascot.

"Whoever took it can keep the bag," Feder said. "We just want the uniform back."

The uniform is worth about $200. It's white with red pinstripes. It has a Toros logo on the front and the name of the mascot on the back.

The name of the mascot is Tuffy. Tuffy's head was not stolen along with the uniform. The head is worth $1,000.

5 Write a summary lead based on the following information, which is from a story in *The Cincinnati Enquirer.*

The DeSales Crossings Center, a 30,000-square-foot building, is the pinnacle of the work of DeSales Crossings, a collaboration of nine partners. It is at St. Francis DeSales Catholic Church at Madison Road and Woodburn Avenue in East Walnut Hills.

The DeSales Crossings Center is the latest in a string of building projects. This project cost $3.1 million. It was dedicated Sunday by Bishop Carol Moeddel, who also blessed the center at the Catholic Church. The building serves as parish center, elementary school offices and a cafeteria.

The center is yet another sign of a neighborhood that is reinventing itself. It is one project that is leading a wider revitalization effort in the neighborhood. Also proposed is a commercial and residential project. Another old school may be turned into 35 loft apartments.

The area is in an inner-city area of Cincinnati.

6 Write a summary lead based on the following information, which is from an Associated Press story.

There has been a police shooting in Hollywood, Fla. A man was killed after an officer fired an M-26 Taser stun gun and hit the man in the chest.

The stun gun shoots probes that transmit 50,000 volts of electricity into the body for up to five seconds.

Police said the man was behaving strangely in from of a hotel. Officers shot him with the stun gun, then wrestled him to the ground and handcuffed him because he had not been subdued.

The man, who police believe was on drugs, refused to get on his knees and put his hands behind his back when police arrived at the hotel Sunday.

When he was shot, the man ripped the darts out of his chest and went after a police officer, a police spokesman said. That's why officers wrestled him to the ground and handcuffed him.

Officers quickly noticed the man was having trouble breathing and called paramedics. When rescue crews arrived, they found the suspect on the ground in handcuffs with no heartbeat. He died at a hospital.

7 Write a summary lead based on the following information, which is from a story in the *Nashville Tennessean.*

There's been a fire on Mapleash Avenue in Columbia, Tenn., which is in Maury County. The Maury County sheriff is Enoch George, and he is the source for the information for this story.

The fire was in a house. It occurred late Saturday. The house exploded and burned.

Three people were killed in the fire. All of those killed were believed to be in their 70s.

Investigators said that the explosion occurred after one of the home's occupants accidentally knocked a propane space heater off a wall.

The wooden-framed house burned quickly. It was fully engulfed in flames when firefighters arrived.

Agents from the state bomb and arson unit were at the scene today sifting for information.

The bodies were taken to Nashville, where the medical examiner will conduct autopsies.

8 Write a summary lead based on the following information from an Associated Press story.

There has been a drought in Marion County in Florida. Since Oct. 1 the central Florida county has experienced a rainfall deficit of five inches.

In addition to a warm autumn, a winter cold spell freese-dried the grass. Now there have been wildfires in the grass.

Last week the wildfires burned 300 acres of grass in Marion County. The region's fire threat remains high for the fourth consecutive year, officials said.

Most of those fires started from illegal burns that were not in approved mesh-covered barrels or pits, she said.

There has been a 32-inch rainfall deficit in the county since the beginning of the drought in April 1998.

Officials have asked residents to stop burning in their backyards until the threat passes.

9 Write a summary lead based on the following information from an Associated Press story.

While there are wildfires in Florida, it's snowing in Washington. There were hundreds of accidents on snow-covered highways in Washington. Icy spots in Oregon caused accidents from Portland to Eugene.

The snowstorm swirled across the Northwest over the weekend.

Fourteen inches of snow fell in some areas. Other areas had 6 inches. The snowfall tapered off by Monday.

At least three people were killed in the weekend snowstorm. A hiker was still missing on Monday. Two of the people were killed in Washington highway accidents. In British Columbia, several hikers got lost in heavy snow. One teenager died and another is missing and presumed dead.

A lot of school districts in western Washington have canceled classes for Monday because of slippery roads. As many as 12,000 electricity customers lost power over the weekend. Flights arriving at Seattle-Tacoma International Airport were delayed an average of two hours Sunday.

10 Write a summary lead based on the following information, which is from a story in *The Tampa* (Fla.) *Tribune.*

Debbie McMillan of south Tampa, Fla., has been sick.

A year ago, the blood vessels feeding her brain ruptured, causing a clot in the back of her head that affected her brain stem.

She had surgery, but she was totally paralyzed and appeared to be in a coma.

Now, 12 months after being on the verge of death, McMillan is running in Saturday's Gasparilla 5K race.

A week after surgery, her toe flickered. She continued to improve.

She's gotten so much better that on Saturday she will run in her first race.

A year ago she looked out her window as the race passed by. To help cheer her up, her doctor told her she would run in the next one. Soon after, she told him she wanted to begin training.

11 Write a summary lead based on the following information, which is from a story in *The Kentucky Post* in northern Kentucky.

The worst part of flu season is yet to come.

Some medical experts had predicted that this year's flu season would be milder than normal.

Not so in northern Kentucky and Cincinnati, where the flu bug has bitten—hard.

In the past two weeks, record numbers of flu and flu-like cases have been reported by area doctors and hospitals.

And things may only get worse.

"It's here, but the worst is yet to come," said Dr. Gilbert Schiff, a flu vaccine researcher at Children's Hospital.

Because of the increase in flu cases, attendance at many schools is well below average. Some schools have closed the past weeks as sick students and teachers suffered headaches, high fevers, vomiting and congestion.

Some hospitals are having trouble finding beds for the most seriously ill.

12 Write a summary lead based on the following information, which is from *The East Valley Tribune,* a daily in suburban Phoenix.

Tempe is planning a series of spring outdoor hikes.

The hikes are being sponsored by the city's Community Services Department.

The first one will be on April 25.

It begins at 9 a.m. at Papago Park.

The hikes are for the disabled.

They are geared for the educable and trainable mentally disabled, age 6 and older, whose physical disabilities do not impair their ability to do physical activities.

Hikes will be about 2 or 3 miles long and will last an hour or two.

The fee is $3.50.

For more information call 555-8381.

13 Write a summary lead based on the following information, which is from a story in *The New York Times.*

Mark Dickson is 24 years old.

He is a student at Stockton State College in New Jersey and had just started working as a disc jockey at a small radio station.

He was shot early today by a man who tried to rob him.

The station is in Vineland, N.J.

Police described the shooting.

They said that Dickson was playing a record at about 1 a.m. on WKQV-FM, a rock'n'roll station, when he heard a knock at the station door.

When he stepped away from his control panel to answer it, he encountered a man holding what appeared to be a revolver.

The assailant demanded money.

Dickson gave him $2 but refused to give up his wallet.

The man fired once, wounding Dickson in the left arm.

He fled, leaving the $2 behind.

Dickson was reported in stable condition in the intensive care unit at Bridgeton Hospital, where he was scheduled to undergo surgery to remove the bullet.

14 Write a summary lead based on the following information, which is from a story in the *Chicago Tribune.*

There are 2,500 students attending Farragut Career Academy High School in Chicago.

The school is at 2345 S. Christiana Ave.

On Friday some of the students began fighting after a scuffle in the lunchroom of the school. The scuffle escalated to gang fights throughout the building.

There were several gang-related fistfights.

Sgt. Frank Hughes of the Marquette Police District said that 20 students were arrested and charged with disorderly conduct. Most of the youths were released on $100 bond, Hughes said.

Three students suffered cuts and bruises and were treated at a local hospital, Principal Steve Newton Jr. said.

Newton said the students at the school were released early on Friday after the gang-related fistfights broke out. They were sent home because staff members at the school decided the commotion was too dangerous to continue classes.

15 Write a summary lead based on the following information, which is from a story by The Associated Press. The story ran in the *Indiana Daily Student.*

This is a Christmas-time story.

There are only 17 days until Christmas, and the Salvation Army is busy with its annual campaign to raise money for the needy.

The bell ringers are out, but the annual Christmas campaign has started slowly in Indianapolis and Fort Wayne.

Scott Justvig, director of development for the Salvation Army, said today that the campaign is about $11,000 short of where it was at the same time last year.

"But it appears things are picking up," he added.

Part of the problem is attributed to the army's exclusion from the two busiest shopping centers in Fort Wayne.

16 Write a summary lead based on the following information, which is from a story in *The Dallas Morning News.*

Archeologists from the University of North Texas, which is in Denton, have been excavating Ray Roberts Lake, which was built as a water supply source for Dallas and Denton.

The lake is also designed for recreation, fishing and wildlife preservation.

The lake was built by the U.S. Army Corps of Engineers. It is north of Denton.

The archeologists are under the direction of Dr. Reid Ferring.

They have excavated Paleo-Indian artifacts that are believed to have been untouched since they were left by the ice age about 12,000 years ago.

On Thursday the carefully guarded site near Ray Roberts Lake will be unveiled by federal officials.

Archeologists are calling the site the most significant find in Texas. It is believed to be the oldest, best-dated and best-preserved example of the ancient Clovis culture in the southern Plains, according to a statement released by the Fort Worth District of the U.S. Army Corps of Engineers.

The prehistoric Clovis culture is known for its fluted stone projectile points. It was named for Clovis, N.M., where such artifacts were first found in 1932. The Clovis people are believed to be the first inhabitants of North America. They were centered primarily in the plateaus and tablelands of New Mexico, Arizona and West Texas.

17 Write a summary lead based on the following information, which is from a story in the *St. Petersburg Times* in Florida.

A 71-year-old woman was walking to her car in the parking lot of Skyway Plaza, near 62nd Avenue S and 10th Street, Sunday afternoon.

According to St. Petersburg Police Sgt. Rollin Lightfield, two men came up to the woman and tried to steal her purse.

The incident occurred shortly before 4 p.m.

The attempt to steal her purse was unsuccessful because the woman refused to hand it over to the two men.

After the unsuccessful attempt, the two men got into a gray Oldsmobile with tinted windows, Lightfield said. He said that as the woman walked to a store for help, the two men drove by her and shot her in the lower back.

The woman then walked into a hardware store, where she asked clerks to call police.

Lightfield said that she was not injured seriously.

18 Write a summary lead based on the following information, which is from a story in the *Albuquerque Journal* in New Mexico.

Michael Wiener, a member of the Albuquerque City Council, has been urging the council to impose a citywide phase-out of plastic bags, which he says can harm the environment.

Wiener says that paper sacks are less dangerous to animals and children, and that they decompose more quickly than plastic.

On Monday the Council voted on Wiener's proposal. It stopped short of banning plastic shopping bags. Instead, the council voted to encourage grocery and retail stores to eliminate the use of plastic bags.

The council voted 8–0 to encourage people to use paper sacks. Members also asked that the mayor study a plan that would require the city to phase out plastic garbage bags.

"I don't think there's enough trees in the world to go back to all paper packaging," Truett Gill told the council before the vote. Gill is the president of the New Mexico Growers Association. He said that he supports voluntary recycling programs but not a ban.

19 Use the following information, which is from a story in the *Chicago Tribune,* to write a summary lead that emphasizes *what.*

Two sacred masks were stolen from the Hopi Indian tribe, and Meryl Pinsoff Platt, 48, an antiquities dealer, was charged in connection with the theft.

She pleaded guilty in November to interstate transportation of stolen property.

The masks are valued at more than $7,000 each.

Platt operates her business out of her home in Wilmette, Ill.

Her sentencing was today in Chicago before U.S. District Judge Milton Shadur.

Shadur fined Platt $6,000. He also sentenced her to 30 days in jail for her role in the sale of the two masks.

She is to serve the sentence on weekends at the federal jail in Chicago, her attorney said.

Platt is cooperating with authorities who are investigating the theft of the sacred masks.

20 Use the following information, which is from an Associated Press story, to write a summary lead that emphasizes *when.*

Martin Marietta has made an announcement concerning the launch of its Titan 3 rocket, which is to boost into orbit communications satellites for a Japanese company and the British Ministry of Defense.

The launch had been scheduled for tonight (Wednesday), but with rain falling throughout the day and with a forecast that stiff upper-level winds would persist for several days, Martin Marietta decided to put off the launch for one week.

The rocket will be launched next Wednesday.

It was the fifth postponement of the launch this month. Three of the scrubs were caused by bad weather.

Liftoff is now scheduled for 7:24 p.m. one week from today.

21 Use the following information, which is from an Associated Press story, to write a summary lead that emphasizes *where.*

Tuesday was a rainy day.

Rain fell on the Midwest, from lower Michigan across northern Indiana and Illinois to northeast Missouri.

It also rained from central Arizona across northwest New Mexico into southern Colorado. And rain extended from the Oregon coast into northwest California.

Rain and thunderstorms are expected to continue Wednesday (today) in the Mississippi Valley, in the central Plains, over the Rockies and in northern Maine.

On Tuesday, it was warm over much of the eastern half of the nation.

In fact, 15 cities set record highs for the date.

22 Use the following information from a story in *The Cincinnati Enquirer* to write a summary lead that emphasizes *who.*

Susan Moisio is a project manager for the Metropolitan Sewer District. She is managing a team that is building a $14 million computer model of the county's sewer system.

She's trying to control a 3,000-mile river running underneath Hamilton County by tracking its ebbs and flows on a computer screen.

It's a river of waste. The job of the Metropolitan Sewer District is to try to contain the flow in more than 45,000 pieces of pipe so that raw sewage doesn't spill into the county's waterways or seep into basements during heavy storms.

Moisio's computer model will become an essential element in how the sewer district settles a decade-long federal pollution lawsuit. A settlement in the suit may be reached and filed in the next two weeks.

The model could provide a graphic image of water flowing through the pipes in real-time so operators can direct water away from full pipes and avoid spills during storms. It also will point out the best areas to build storage in the system.

Her model will help the system when it's time to build a $10 million sewer system, which is needed because the sewer district is under pressure from the federal government to eliminate overflows.

23 The following lead, which is from a story in the *Chicago Tribune,* contains 50 words. Pare it to an acceptable length.

U.S. District Judge Prentice Marshall has issued a preliminary injunction preventing Michael Narcum, of Woodstock, from receiving mail on behalf of an allegedly bogus company called International Success Development/Commission of Mailers of North America, through which he is suspected of bilking hundreds of people out of more than $80,000.

24 Use the following information to write a multiple-element lead.

There was a hit-and-run accident in town Monday night.

It occurred on First Street, just west of Central Street.

The source for the story is police spokesman Roger Clinton.

A 3-year-old boy, Jonathan M. Beltran, who lived with his parents at 101 W. First St., was struck and killed.

His parents are Robert and Louise Beltran.

The boy was dead at the scene from head injuries, Clinton said.

About an hour later, Butler Adamson, 22, of 1616 W. Eighth St., called police and admitted that he struck the child as the toddler was crossing First Street.

Adamson was arrested and charged with leaving the scene of an accident.

Adamson, who works at an auto-parts store on Central Street, was booked into City Jail Monday night and released on his own recognizance Tuesday morning after appearing in Justice Court.

A preliminary hearing on a charge of leaving the scene of an accident involving death has been set for May 15.

25 The lead in the following story is buried. Find the most important points of the story, and then rewrite the lead.

The FBI has been investigating the First National Bank after bank officials reported that more than $450,000 turned up missing during a routine bank audit.

The investigation has been going on for the last two weeks.

Bank officials said that they believe the embezzlement scheme involved electronic transfers of money over a period of time.

Late Wednesday, Roger Dubin, bank president, confirmed that a 31-year-old officer of the bank had been fired in the alleged embezzlement scheme.

Dubin said that the officer is cooperating with authorities, and more arrests will follow.

The FBI refused to comment on the case.

First National Bank is the city's largest.

26 Read the following story, which is from *The East Valley Tribune* in suburban Phoenix. Rewrite the lead into six different leads that emphasize, respectively, (a) *who,* (b) *what,* (c) *where,* (d) *when,* (e) *why* and (f) *how.*

The best way to drive through a construction zone is—don't.

That's what experts said motorists should do to avoid damage to their cars.

"Go out of your way to avoid it if you have to," said Dave Benyl, a claims and insurance manager for Tanner Companies, which has a contract to improve Chandler Boulevard from Kyrene Road to Dobson Road. "We have 20,000 cars a day pass over the construction. Some of the older cars can't withstand the bumps."

Construction on 8 1/2 miles of Chandler Boulevard between Interstate 10 and Dakota Street is the largest road improvement district ever attempted in the state.

The $20 million project, which began in early January, is scheduled for completion in June.

Jim Conway, a mechanic at Freeway Mobil, at I-10 and Chandler Boulevard, said he repairs flat tires all day. But he said there is no way to avoid running over screws, chunks of metal or nails, the most common of the tire hazards.

"You're not going to see a nail in the road," he said. "You're just not going to be able to steer around that."

Mike Elliot, vice president of Nesbitt Contracting Co., which has a contract to improve Chandler Boulevard from I-10 to Kyrene and from Dobson to Dakota, said he hears complaints from people who want to be reimbursed for car damage from the construction.

"We take every claim in writing and then we go out and evaluate each claim individually," Elliot said. "We check to see if the warning signs were up or if we left the area in a dangerous situation."

Elliot said he hasn't paid anyone yet for damages from Chandler Boulevard construction.

"It's hard to prove," he said. "Sometimes people want us to pay for new tires or to align their vehicle. But we have no idea if they got the nail on our road or somewhere else. They have to prove that we were grossly negligent."

Elliot said people should drive the maximum of 25 mph or even slower in all construction sites.

Benyl said he also gets complaints.

"Normally we don't leave nails on the road," he said.

He said the best solution would be to have no one drive in the construction areas. "It would be nice if we could shut down the whole area," he said. "We could do the job a lot faster and a lot less expensively. No one would be running over rocks."

5

Special Leads

Review Questions

1 The narrative lead is the most popular lead in features and non-breaking news stories. Explain what it is, and give two examples from newspapers.

2 What is a nut graph? Give an example from a feature story.

3 Explain observation. Why is it important in a story?

4 Explain what a contrast lead is, and give two examples.

5 What part do turn words play in contrast leads? Give two creative examples.

6 What is a staccato lead? Give two examples.

7 Explain what a direct-address lead is, and give two examples.

8 Why should a direct-address lead be used sparingly?

9 Explain what a question lead is, and give two examples.

10 What is a quote lead? Give two examples.

11 Why do editors so often ban question and quote leads?

12 What are guidelines for writing a quote lead?

13 What is a "none of the above" lead? Give two examples.

14 Why are vivid verbs so important in writing? Give examples from newspapers of five leads that use vivid verbs.

Suggested Exercises

1 Any one of the special leads could have been used in the following story, which starts with a summary lead. (Much of the information is from a weather story in the *Chicago Tribune.*) Read the story, and then top it with the following leads: (a) narrative, (b) contrast, (c) staccato, (d) direct address, (e) question, (f) quote and (g) "none of the above."

Temperatures in the city and across the Midwest powered past the 80-degree mark, shattering records on the way.

It was 88 here at 4:15 p.m. Saturday, the warmest March 22 ever. Last year on the same date, the high was 33.

Joining the city in record warmth were, among other cities, Milwaukee, Minneapolis and Des Moines.

Though temperatures are expected to drop into the low 70s today, meteorologists are predicting continuing sunshine.

Throughout the city, people took advantage of the heat to de-mothball the tank tops, tune up the 10-speeds and head out to a park. Those lucky enough to own convertibles put down the tops and went out for a weekend drive.

Students at City University even sunbathed at Olive Park Beach, right under the sign that read, "Beach Officially Closed Until June 1."

Most everybody on campus was outside somewhere, whether talking on the lawns or roller skating along cement walkways. The most popular activity was hanging around the beach.

"Suntan 101 meets from 1:30 to 3:30 every day," said sun culturist Brad Smith from Atlanta. "Bring your suntan lotion and a bottle of beer."

Beer seemed to be the preferred beverage of the day.

"There's nothing like a cold one on a warm day," shouted Cindy Weiss, a 22-year-old waitress who took a day off to spend at the beach. "These days come so seldom."

2 Use the following information, which is from a story in *The Arizona Republic* in Phoenix, to write a narrative lead.

The Chandler Ostrich Festival was held Saturday in Chandler, a city in the metropolitan Phoenix area. Your story is being written for the Sunday paper.

The racecourse is 100 yards long.

More than 1,000 spectators attended the festival.

Joe Hedrick of Nickerson, Kan., owns the birds that participated in the festival. The birds weigh as much as 400 pounds each.

Hedrick said that he is one of only two people in the country offering ostrich races to the public. He brought nine birds for the Chandler Festival.

The riders race bareback on the birds. In one race, a bird fell on its rider, another rider fell off his bird and one bird returned to the starting gate.

Sylvester the ostrich won one race. Before the race he stretched his legs and eyed his opponents.

A yellow flag signaled the start of the race. When the yellow flag fell, Sylvester looked at the spectators and then bolted forward as fast as his long, muscular legs would carry him.

Sylvester has been racing for seven years.

In this race, he took an early lead. He hugged the inside lane and never broke stride.

The race took him only seconds to win. He made it to the finish line 25 yards ahead of the second-place bird.

The Chandler Festival continues from 10 a.m. to 8 p.m. on Sunday. The festivities include a chili cook-off, art auction and jazz performance.

3 Use the following information, which is from a story in the *Iowa State Daily* at Iowa State University, to write a narrative lead.

Rick is 27 years old. He makes his living repossessing cars. The work is often unpleasant and occasionally dangerous, but that does not bother Rick. He's athletic, the kind of guy you would want on your side in a fight.

This story will refer to the main source by first name only because many people dislike a "repo man."

Rick has a tanned face, dark curly hair and a long nose. He has a scar above his left eyebrow, the souvenir of a run-in with an angry debtor.

Rick's job begins when he is hired by a bank to repossess a car from a buyer who is far behind on the payments. For example, here is how he handled a job for a bank in Des Moines.

First, he gets a letter, an "Assignment for Repossession," from the bank. The assignment includes the borrower's name, a copy of the vehicle's registration, the type of vehicle, key numbers and a copy of the loan-payment record.

The car is a Chevrolet Celebrity. The borrower is three months behind on his payments. The payment record shows an unpaid balance of $10,056.55.

Under "additional comments" is written:

"WIFE—TAMARA—
PROBABLY DRIVING CAR—
WORKS McDONALD'S DAYS—
IN INDIANOLA."

Next, Rick calls the McDonald's. "Is Tamara there?" he asks. "OK, thank you." He is put on hold. In a few minutes he is told no, Tamara isn't there right now, but she is scheduled to work at 11. Rick hangs up. He's ready to go to work.

Rick heads for the McDonald's during the lunch-hour rush. He drives his Renault Alliance into the parking lot. He glances at the official paper in his hand and asks, "What color is it?" The paper tells him. "OK, that's it right there," he says, pointing to the Celebrity. He tells his passenger, "I'll just have you get behind the wheel of this one and follow me back to town."

Next, Rick opens the door of his car, glances into the restaurant and walks briskly to the Celebrity. He produces a pick from a packet in his hand. He gets inside the car and slides back the seat. There's the sound of an engine starting, and Rick drives the Celebrity out of the lot.

It takes less than 20 seconds. If you blinked your eyes, you missed it.

"See, that was easier than your average repo," Rick said later. "It was just a matter of getting in and driving off. She was at work, she couldn't see out. It she did, she saw me leaving the lot, but at that point I'm already gone and it's too late.

"It's not like taking a car out of somebody's driveway. Every once in a while you get somebody who's half goofy in the head. You gotta be careful because a lot of these people are professional deadbeats. And once a deadbeat, always a deadbeat."

4 Use the following information, which is from a story in the *Hastings* (Neb.) *Tribune,* to write a contrast lead.

Dan Bryan was sworn in as district county judge for Fillmore, Saline, Thayer and Nuckolls counties last month. He was appointed to the position after Judge Ray Cellar retired.

Bryan and Cellar are from Geneva, Neb.

Bryan is no stranger to the court. For 15 years he was prosecuting cases as the Fillmore County attorney.

Bryan graduated from Creighton University. He is 39 years old.

He started hearing civil cases this month, but he probably won't be hearing any criminal cases in Fillmore County for about a year because he has to complete his affairs as county attorney first.

Then he won't be prosecuting cases. Instead, he will spend most of his time listening and making decisions.

The Fillmore County Board appointed Bryan's law partner as the county attorney.

Bryan said that in his new position, he'll "have to learn to keep my mouth shut and listen."

5 Use the following information, which is from an Associated Press story that appeared in *The Arizona Daily Star* in Tucson, to write a contrast lead.

Patrick Hogan's left leg was amputated three years ago. He had complications from diabetes. Hogan is a retired radio announcer.

His shoe size is 13-D. After the amputation, Hogan's need for shoes changed forever. He realized that in order to buy new shoes, he had to pay full price for a pair and then throw the left one into a growing pile in the back of his closet.

One day, Hogan was thumbing through the phone book and he came across the National Odd Shoe Exchange in Phoenix. That's when his luck changed.

The non-profit agency has been around since 1943, serving people with two different-size feet or, like Hogan, with only one foot.

The organization is called NOSE. Its cramped offices overflow with more than one million shoes donated by more than two dozen manufacturers. It serves 17,000 people in the United States and Canada.

6 Use the following information, which is from the *Buffalo* (N.Y.) *News,* to write a staccato lead.

Americans don't know a lot about Afganistan, particularly its food and cooking.

The country is slightly smaller than Texas. It is in south central Asia and is semi-arid and landlocked. It has few forests and is unable to produce many crops.

Here are some more things about Afganistan. It has barren sands. The summers are hot. The winters are cold and harsh.

But the nation's food, drink and culinary traditions are lush. And many of the traditions are adopted from Afganistan's neighbors.

The country's food uses mainly fresh ingredients and powerful spices.

People there don't use a lot of spices—and no curries at all—but they rely on mint, saffron, cardamom and tumeric.

One favorite dish is aashak, which is teamed scallion-filled dumplings topped with spicy meat sauce and yogurt. Then it is sprinkled with mint.

The staple is nuts, including pistachios and almonds. Lamb, chicken and beef are used in dishes.

7 Use the following information, which is from a story in the *Birmingham* (Ala.) *Post-Herald,* to write a direct-address lead.

The body can be used for fast, approximate measuring. For example:

- The first joint of an index finger is 1 inch long.
- The span of a wide-spread hand, from the tip of the thumb to the tip of the pinkie, is about 9 inches.
- The distance from the elbow to the tip of middle finger is about 18 inches.

Need a ruler? Look in a wallet:

- Laid out flat, a dollar bill is 6¼ inches long.
- Folded in half, it is 3 inches.
- Folded in half again, it is 1½ inches.
- A penny is three-fourths of an inch across.
- A standard paper clip is 1¼ inches long; a giant clip is 1 inches long.

These tips can help people do the job without rulers when they don't always have the best measuring tools on hand.

8 Use the following information, which is from a story in *The Times-Picayune* in New Orleans, to write a direct-address lead.

This story is a travel piece about Costa Rica, the Central American country south of Nicaragua and north of Panama.

Costa Rica contains flora and fauna characteristic of both North and South America. It has 12,000 varieties of plants, 237 species of mammals, 848 kinds of birds and 361 types of amphibians and reptiles.

The country is about the size of West Virginia.

Much of the plant and animal life is protected by the Costa Rican national park system.

There is a lot to do in Costa Rica:

- Swim with angel fish and sunbathe with iguanas.
- Look down on the clouds or up at a troop of monkeys.
- Look out at a flock of bright green parrots.
- Enjoy the air-conditioned deluxe accommodations.
- Visit parks that have admission costs of generally less than 50 cents per person.
- Tour beaches, mountains or both.
- Tour the Paos volcano, which is 9,000 feet above sea level and is an active volcano, accessible by a good road.

Costa Rica is bordered by the Pacific Ocean on the west and the Caribbean Sea on the east. It is divided by four mountain ranges.

San José is the country's capital. It is the largest city in Costa Rica and is home to the country's largest airport.

9 Use the following information, which is from a story in the *Indiana Daily Student* at Indiana University, to write a question lead.

For those students tired of trudging all the way across campus every morning to get to class, the university is going to bring the classes to them.

Next fall nearly 100 classes will be taught in residence halls to about 2,500 students. Classes range from introduction to computer programming to culture and society.

The residential education classes to be offered in the fall are about a 12 percent increase over the number available this year.

This summer the conference room in Ashton Center will be converted into a combination classroom/conference room, said Larry Gaffney, halls of residence director. He added that other residence hall–classroom facilities will be painted and will receive new blackboards.

By August, every dorm on campus will have at least one classroom and several will have more, said Nancy Lorenz, assistant to the dean of students for residential education.

Along with more convenient class locations, benefits of the residence hall–classroom program include smaller classes, help sessions and easy access to instructors, Lorenz said.

But there are some flaws, too, she said. If a student has another class away from his hall, he may have problems getting from one class to another in time.

10 Use the following information, which is from a story in *The Arizona Republic* in Phoenix, to write a quote lead.

This is a story about Melissa Martinez, an artist who also works for the Scottsdale Museum of Modern Art. Her job is to lead the installation of millions of dollars of art that rotates through the museum each year.

She's 26 years old and not like the typical person doing such work in a museum. The typical person would be older and male.

Her job title is "preparator."

"Sometimes I feel like I should be introducing myself as a 40-year-old man," she says.

She likes to do installations that provide a sense of the artist's working style and says that sometimes artists look at her as though she is not up for the job. But once they see her operate a forklift, hang plaster board or use a crowbar on a crate, they know that she can fill bare walls and floors.

"If I had to do anything besides making art, this would be it," Martinez says. She has an art degree in sculpture and is working on a show of her own.

11 Use the following information, which is from a story in the *Daily Forty-Niner* at California State University, Long Beach, to write a "none of the above" lead.

This story is about an 18th-century ballad opera called "The Beggar's Opera," which is playing for the second weekend at the University Theatre.

It's a jolly ole show with more than its fair share of roguish highwaymen and damsels, most of whom aren't particularly in distress.

The opera was written by John Gay and updated in the 20th century by Benjamin Britten. It is a burlesque of more maudlin operas.

The main characters are the Peachums, a family of thieves and whores.

Mr. Peachum, played by Kenneth Church, seems genteel, but he's really an expert pickpocket. He's a scoundrel, but he's also devoted to his daughter and wife.

Mrs. Peachum (Deborah Day) is graciously evil, for she sweetly tells Mr. Peachum, "You know, my dear, I never meddle in matters of death. I leave that to you."

When she's not pickpocketing or conniving with her husband, Mrs. Peachum is usually reprimanding her daughter, Polly

(Stephanie Vlahos), about some imagined sin. She's always calling Polly a slut or a hussy.

But Polly is no slut or hussy. She emerges from this family as "normal," much like the niece of "The Munsters," a 1960s television sitcom.

All of the action takes place on a stage with ropes, stone stairs and open ceilings with low-hanging sheets, creating a merry, musty England effect. It all adds to the pun.

The action begins at 8 p.m. and runs through March 15, Tickets are $4.50 on Thursday and $7.50 on Friday and Saturday.

12 History was made when the U.S. Senate acquitted President Bill Clinton of perjury and obstruction of justice in his impeachment trial. Presiding over the trial was U.S. Supreme Court Chief Justice William H. Rehnquist. After the trial ended, The Associated Press transmitted a story about Rehnquist by writer Laurie Asseo.

The story follows. After you have read it, try rewriting the summary lead into a lead block, using one of the special leads discussed in this chapter.

You must use the information contained in the story. Don't make up anything.

WASHINGTON (AP)—Presiding over the Senate trial was a bit of a "culture shock," Chief Justice William H. Rehnquist said Friday as he completed his duties as only the second chief justice to oversee a presidential impeachment trial.

"I leave you now a wiser, but not a sadder, man," Rehnquist told senators shortly after pronouncing President Clinton "not guilty as charged" on both impeachment articles.

The Senate gave Rehnquist a standing ovation and a golden gavel on a plaque, and Majority Leader Trent Lott thanked him for lending the proceedings "a gentle dignity and an unfailing sense of purpose and sometimes a sense of humor."

"Y'all come back soon, but I hope that's not taken the wrong way and not for an occasion like this one," said Lott, R–Miss.

Rehnquist, who is used to presiding over the Supreme Court's non-televised proceedings, noted, "I was a stranger to the great majority of you" when he came to the Senate in January. "I underwent the sort of culture shock that naturally occurs when one moves from the very structured (environment) of the Supreme Court to what I shall call, for want of a better phrase, the more freeform environment of the Senate," he said, causing the senators to break into laughter.

He said he was impressed with Senate leaders' ability to agree on procedural rules and by "the quality of the debate in closed session."

"Our work as a court of impeachment is now done," Rehnquist said. "I leave you with the hope that our several paths may cross again, under happier circumstances."

6

Organizing a News Story

Review Questions

1 Explain an inverted pyramid. What should be in the lead? In the body? At the end? Give an example of an inverted pyramid.

2 What are the steps to follow in organizing an inverted pyramid?

3 What is transition? How is it used? Give four examples of transition from newspaper stories.

4 Explain the hourglass style of news writing. On what type of stories is it best used?

5 What are the advantages of the hourglass style?

6 Explain the circle style writing form.

7 What are the advantages of writing in a circle?

Suggested Exercises

1 Here is a nine-paragraph story from The Associated Press, but the paragraphs are not in the order they were in when the story was published. Organize the paragraphs into a readable story. The dateline on the story is BAGHDAD, Iraq.

The United States has accused Iraq of more than 90 violations of the no-fly zones since mid-December. It said U.S. and British forces have retaliated by attacking more than 40 Iraqi targets.

Both Kuwait and Saudi Arabia have opened their air bases to U.S. and British planes that patrol the no-fly zones.

The zones were set up by the United States, Britain and France after the 1991 Persian Gulf War to prevent the Iraqi air force from attacking rebels in the north and south.

"We, by help from God and support from the sons of our glorious Arab nation, including true and sincere nationals … in Saudi Arabia and Kuwait, have the ability to attack the soldiers and means of aggression from whatever region," Iraqi television said, quoting a statement from President Saddam Hussein and senior leaders.

"Once again … we draw the attention of the rulers of Saudi Arabia and Kuwait and tell them you are getting involved now in a vicious and aggressive war that the people of Saudi Arabia and Kuwait have no interest in," the statement said.

The statement did not specify what type of action Iraq would take against the U.S. and British bases.

The Iraqi government said Sunday it

could attack American and British bases in the Persian Gulf that are used to launch airstrikes against Iraq.

The Iraqi statement was issued following a meeting Saddam held with three senior aides. It again warned Saudi Arabia and Kuwait to distance themselves from the United States.

The statement came amid a simmering war of nerves with the United States and Britain over "no-fly" zones imposed in northern and southern Iraq. Iraq does not recognize the zones and has vowed to fire at any plane that violates its airspace.

2 Here is a seven-paragraph story from The Associated Press, but the paragraphs are not in the order they were in when the story was published. Organize the paragraphs into a readable story. The dateline on the story is NEWARK, N.J. You probably will have to rewrite the opening paragraphs of your story to insert the suspect's full name.

Authorities say Manuel Febus has been married more than 11 times. But the Romeo allegedly wasn't promising eternal love, just a green card.

The New Yorker makes Elizabeth Taylor look like a novice when it comes to marriage.

The serial bridegroom, who is free on $50,000 bail, has no listed number, and his lawyer did not return calls.

In at least one case, he allegedly charged a fee. A woman married Febus on Valentine's Day 1997 after agreeing to pay $5,500 to an associate of Febus to find her a husband, according to court papers.

"If you file photographs of yourself, eventually you're going to get caught," immigration lawyer Melvin R. Solomon said.

Nearly all of the brides submitted a photo of themselves with Febus as part of their applications to the Immigration and Naturalization Service.

He was accused in federal court last month of illegally helping immigrant women gain permanent residency by marrying them.

3 Here is an 11-paragraph story from the *Daily Bruin* at UCLA, but the paragraphs are not in the order they were in when the story was published. Organize the paragraphs into a readable story.

"Westwood has become a beacon that attracts people who have nothing to do," said Sgt. John Bradbury of the West Los Angeles Police Department. "Minors cause problems with overcrowding, drinking, drugs and fighting."

Minors loitering in the village after 10 p.m. will be cited for violation of the curfew. Offenders are taken to the police station and usually released into their parents' custody, Bradbury said, adding that repeat offenders can be brought to juvenile court.

"This rarely happens," Bradbury said. "Usually once is enough."

"Hopefully with all this activity," Bradbury added, "we will make Westwood safer and more accessible to those people who have a purpose for being there."

As summer vacation approaches, the West Los Angeles Police Department will implement extra security measures to combat problems with overcrowding and loitering in Westwood.

Beginning the first weekend in May, West LAPD will resume periodic curfew sweeps and mounted patrols, said Linda Arneal, coordinator of the Westwood Village Merchants Association.

Curfew sweeps will be periodic so that people will not know when they are coming, Arneal said.

Summer security measures are being implemented earlier this year as a precaution, Arneal said.

"The merchants are concerned with keeping the older crowds around because they're the ones that spend the money," Arneal said. "The police are aware of the problems in Westwood, and they are very helpful in cooperating with us."

Arneal added that officers on horseback are part of a special task force designed to increase security and ensure the safety of Westwood Village merchants and visitors.

"These policies were very successful last year," Arneal added. "As long as they continue to serve their purposes they will be maintained."

4 Use the following information to write a news story in the hourglass style.

There was a protest on campus Friday, and 22 people were arrested. Three university police officers were also injured.

More than 200 demonstrators—most of them students—were on campus during the Board of Regents meeting. One of the items on the regents' agenda was the university's plan to require a class in cultural diversity for all faculty.

The protest was organized by two newly formed campus groups, Students Against Racism and the American Student Organization.

All of the 22 arrested were students. Twenty-one were taken to County Jail. Their attorney, Susan J. Keegan, said that she expected bail to be set at $500 apiece. The 22nd student, a 17-year-old high school senior, was released into his parents' custody.

All of those arrested were charged with trespassing on state property after they refused to disperse. Twelve were also charged with resisting arrest. Ten were charged with assault after they allegedly threw rocks and bottles at university police officers.

"It just got out of hand," said University Police Chief R. Barclay Peterson. "First they were gathered around the fountain at Central Mall. One group was chanting, 'No more racism' and the other was saying 'Stop diversity.' Then they started marching toward Regents Hall, where the regents were meeting. They were disrupting classes. When they were asked to disperse, all hell broke loose."

Peterson said he did not call extra officers in until the protesters started marching. Then, about 60 police officers, two of them on horseback, started toward the demonstrators.

"They should not have come at us," said Jonathan Walterson, president of Students Against Racism. "We would have remained loud, but peaceful. We were doing what we believed in. The university must do more to promote diversity."

Walterson, a junior journalism student, was one of those arrested. He was charged with assault, resisting arrest and trespassing.

Peterson said that his three officers were injured when they were hit by stones or bottles.

Officer Andrea Wilson was taken to Good Samaritan Hospital with a gash on her forehead. She was the first officer hit, Peterson said. Officer James Nelson and Sgt. Jerico Turner were taken to Community Hospital with bruises they received from thrown items, Peterson added.

Peterson said the two groups began a rally at noon. The regents had been meeting since 8 a.m. and were on their lunch break in the Student Union from noon to 1:30 p.m. The first item on their afternoon agenda was the class requirement. Currently, students must take a class in diversity, but faculty do not.

At about 1:15 p.m., protesters from both groups started marching to Regents Hall, where they hoped to meet the regents at the steps as the officials returned from lunch, Peterson said.

They never made it to Regents Hall.

Peterson said he called in the extra officers at about 1:20 p.m. because "the demonstrators just got too loud and rowdy. We asked them several times to disperse and go back to the fountain, where the rally was to be held, but they would not. They shouted at each other even louder, and some of them began throwing things."

Until extra officers were called in, there were a half dozen officers watching the two groups. They were about 25 yards away.

Peterson said that the protesters were stopped midway between the fountain and Regents Hall, near the Liberal Arts Building.

He said that officers using bullhorns ordered the demonstrators to disperse.

Peterson said that the demonstrators refused.

By 1:25 p.m., the demonstration was at its worst, Peterson said. That's when most of the protesters started shouting directly at the police and began throwing things at them, Peterson added.

Officer Wilson was hit in the head about that time, Peterson said.

He said that by 1:30 p.m., most of the demonstrators began to back off. Those who did not were arrested, he added.

Peterson said that the two officers on horseback were used to push back the crowds. "The horses worked well," he said. "The demonstrators were not afraid to push police officers, but they couldn't push the horses."

Peterson said that the protest delayed the beginning of the afternoon session of the regents meeting. The regents stayed in the Student Union until about 2 p.m. and then returned to Regents Hall, he said.

The regents did not take action on the new requirement. They decided to study the matter more and discuss it again at their next monthly meeting, which will be held May 16 in Regents Hall.

"We will continue protesting until the regents vote to mandate faculty training," Walterson said. "We're done negotiating with them. Now it is time to cause trouble." Walterson said that there will be more rallies, not only at the next regents meeting but before then.

"We're not against rallies," Peterson said. "They can hold them all they want, as long as they get a permit from the university. But we don't want them to get out of hand. We don't want our officers hurt. They can rally, but other peaceful students also have the right to attend classes without being disrupted by shouting and violent demonstrators."

The regents refused to comment on why they took no action Friday. "Until we make our decision on faculty training, we will not discuss it," said regents president Clifford Eisel.

Brian Allen, a senior biology student and president of the American Student Organization, said his group will continue protesting, too.

"We'll do whatever it takes to keep the regents from caving into every demand that comes along," he said. "Our faculty do not need additional training in diversity. Many of our faculty aren't even from this country."

Allen was one of the students arrested and charged with assault, resisting arrest and trespassing. Thirteen of those arrested were from his group.

"The two groups never began fighting, but they kept screaming at each other as though they would begin a brawl at any second," Peterson said. "There never would have been a problem if they simply would have moved back when we asked them. Instead, both groups decided to gang up against the police."

5 Use the following information, which is from a story by The Associated Press, to write an inverted pyramid news story. The dateline on the story should be TAYLORSVILLE, N.C.

There has been a fire in a house. The house is in Taylorsville, N.C., which is located about 50 miles west of Winston-Salem. Taylorsville is in Alexander County.

The fire's cause was not immediately known. You got this information from Patricia Lee of the Alexander County Communications Center.

Six people were killed when the fire tore through the house. Officials said a newborn baby was among the dead.

You also interviewed a neighbor, John McWhorter. He told you that a woman living in the one-story brick house ran to his home to call 911 about 4 a.m.

The dead reportedly were aged 2 days to 20 years.

McWhorter told you that the woman told him that six other people were in the house.

Here's a quote from McWhorter: "When I got up there, it was burning so bad, I mean you couldn't even get close to that house. The heat was something fierce."

McWhorter also told you that Ronnie Shue's family lived in the house. He said Shue was called home from his third-shift job.

Here's another quote from McWhorter: "He (Shue) came home and I tried to calm him down, of course. Then the EMS people carried him and her off."

7

Developing a News Story

Review Questions

1 What factors determine if a story is developed from day to day?

2 What are the four phases of a developing story? Give examples of a story in each of the phases.

3 Why is it important to advance each story that is written from day to day during coverage of a developing event? Why is it important to provide adequate background in each story?

4 Why is color important in developing stories?

Suggested Exercises

1 Use the following information to write a breaking news story. Use your town as the *where* of the story. The time element is Tuesday night.

Police are reporting that a 4-year-old child is missing. Her name is Angela Melissa Norton and she lives with her parents at 2346 N. 17th Ave.

Her parents are Samuel R. and Maria L. Norton, who also live at the 17th Avenue address.

The Nortons had gone to dinner and a movie Tuesday evening and had left the child in the care of a 16-year-old baby sitter by the name of Nancy Bonner. Nancy is a high school sophomore. She lives with her parents at 2439 N. 17th Ave.

When the Nortons got home from the show, Nancy was asleep on the living room couch instead of being awake and watching the child. The Nortons went into the child's bedroom and she was not in her crib.

They called police, who have begun searching for the child.

Here is a quote from local police Sgt. Timothy McClung, who is a public information officer. "All we know right now is that the baby sitter says she put the child to sleep at 9 p.m. When the parents got home at 10:30 p.m. the child was not in the house and the baby sitter was asleep on the couch. We are asking anyone who might have some information on the child to please call the police department. We don't need your name, but we sure need your help."

Police said that when she was last seen, Angela was wearing pajamas with Mickey Mouse images printed on them. She has light brown curly hair.

Samuel R. Norton is a senior partner in the local law firm of Norton, Smith and Taylor.

2 Use the following information to write a second-day story on missing Angela Melissa Norton.

It has been 24 hours since she was found to be missing. Police still are questioning the baby sitter and the parents.

There really is nothing new to report except that police have knocked on every door in the six-block area around the Norton house in the last 24 hours, asking neighbors if they might have seen or heard something.

Maria L. Norton, the mother, met with reporters gathered outside the home. She issued the following statement:

"We are begging anyone who might have seen our daughter to please call the police or us. She has never been away from home without us, and we are certain that she must be terrified not to be in her own home. Please, anyone who has information, please let us know."

3 Use the following information to write a Saturday morning story on the missing child in your town.

It turns out that the baby sitter and her boyfriend kidnapped 4-year-old Angela Norton.

The boyfriend is 17-year-old Jonathan Matthew Presley, who lives with his parents at 1970 W. Franklin St. Presley is a junior at the same high school that Nancy Bonner attends.

Sgt. Timothy McClung said the baby sitter admitted to police during questioning that she and her boyfriend kidnapped the child Tuesday night in an effort to collect ransom from the Nortons. He said that Bonner faked being asleep when the Nortons returned home and found their daughter missing.

"The baby sitter did not figure on the Nortons calling the police right away," McClung said. "She thought they would just be frantic until her boyfriend called them anonymously at 11 p.m. to tell them that the child would be safe if they had the baby sitter deliver $25,000 to him. Problem is, these kids didn't do much thinking at all. The parents got home earlier than expected and called police right away. Officers were already at the house when the kidnapper called. We did not tell reporters what we knew the night of the kidnapping because we did not want to jeopardize the return of the child."

McClung said the child was not returned to her home until three days after the kidnapping because police officers could not find Presley, who took the girl to a local motel and hoped that he could collect a ransom even after the plot failed.

"When he was arrested, he told police he turned himself in with the child because he was tired of her crying," McClung said.

The child was returned safely to her parents this morning after spending three nights in the motel. She was not harmed, although she was hungry and dirty.

Presley and Bonner have been referred to juvenile authorities, who say that kidnapping charges will be filed against the two.

8

Quotations and Attribution

Review Questions

1 List three types of quotations that reporters can use in their stories.

2 List five instances in which direct quotations might logically be used in stories.

3 List five pitfalls to avoid when quoting sources.

4 Discuss Associated Press style on the use of profanity in direct quotations.

5 Discuss Associated Press style on the use of dialect in direct quotations.

6 List 10 verbs of attribution.

7 Explain why the sentence preceding a broadcast soundbite should be a *blind lead-in.*

8 Explain why the word *said* is the most common verb of attribution.

9 Discuss the following conventions, which apply to the use of material.

a On the record

b Off the record

c On background

d On deep background

10 Discuss the pros and cons of using anonymous sources.

11 Discuss the handling of quotes from e-mail sources.

Suggested Exercises

1 Read stories on the front page of your local daily newspaper. Select three examples of complete direct quotations. List them.

2 Select three examples of partial quotations. List them.

3 Select three examples of indirect or paraphrased quotations. List them.

4 Clip five stories from your local daily. Examine the direct and indirect quotations used in them. Do you agree with the way in which the quotations were handled? Are unnecessary direct quotations used? Are more needed?

5 Clip three stories from your local daily that contain several direct and indirect quotations. Underline the verbs of attribution. Is *said* the dominant verb of attribution?

6 In the three stories that you clipped for exercise 5, circle the various placements of attribution. Would you have placed any of them differently? Give examples.

7 Insert proper punctuation and capitalization or correct existing punctuation and capitalization in the following sentences.

a “A new football coach will be hired by Friday, said athletic director Cliff Gibson.

b “This is a great day for Geneva”, said Mayor Johnson.

c According to Smith, there are several “first-rate prospects:” Charles Mays; Richard Kile; John Harig and Stanley Kelly.

d The teacher asked, “What is the capital of Delaware”?

e John wondered why every teacher “always expects us to know all the state capitals?”

f “My professor quoted Benvolio from ‘Romeo and Juliet’ who said, “Why, Romeo, art thou mad?” said Susan.

g “The president will hold a press conference Thursday evening at 6 o’clock.” said Johnson.

h “The problem,” Smith said, “Is that nobody seems to know what is happening.

i Smith said, “Journalists often work long hours. However, the extra hours are worth it if a solid story can be gained. The best journalists are more than willing to take the extra time.”

8 President George W. Bush and His Majesty King Abdullah of Jordan participated in a photo opportunity in the Oval Office less than a month after hijackers crashed two airliners into the World Trade Center in New York, a third plane hit the Pentagon and a fourth crashed in rural Pennsylvania. They made opening remarks and then took questions. (a) Underline the statements that are most worthy of direct quotation. Defend your selections. (b) Circle statements that you would use as indirect quotations or paraphrases in a story. Defend your selections. (c) Rewrite the statements that you circled for exercise *b* as indirect quotations or paraphrases.

President Bush: Your Majesty, welcome back.

King Abdullah: Thank you.

President Bush: It's great to see you. I look forward to our discussions. Jordan is a strong, strong friend of America. And right after September 11th, one of the early messages I received was from His Majesty, expressing the condolences of the Jordanian people, as well as his own personal condolences.

I'm so pleased with our cooperative—the cooperation we have in fighting terror. I have assured His Majesty that our war is against evil, not against Islam. There are thousands of Muslims who proudly call themselves Americans, and they know what I know—that the Muslim faith is based upon peace and love and compassion. The exact opposite of the teachings of the al Qaeda organization, which is based upon evil and hate and destruction.

And finally, as a welcoming gift, it is my honor to present you with a pen. This is no ordinary pen, since it's the pen I used to sign the Free Trade Agreement with Jordan this morning. At long last, we have, together, accomplished one of your main objectives in terms of economic cooperation, which is the Free Trade Agreement.

I'm proud of the actions of our leadership in the House and the Senate from both political parties that recognize the importance of trade with Jordan. And so, Your Majesty, it's now officially the law, and here's the pen that signed it.

King Abdullah: Thank you very much, sir. Very grateful

President Bush: Welcome back to the Oval Office.

King Abdullah: Sir, I would like to take this opportunity to thank you for seeing us today. Obviously, I wish our meeting was under better circumstances, but obviously, we're here to give our full, unequivocal support to you and to the people of America. And we will stand by you in these very difficult times. And we're proud of our friendship; we're proud of the relations we've had with your country over many, many years, as far back as his late Majesty King Hussein.

And it's in difficult times like this that true friends must stand with each other, and we'll be by your side and we'll be there to support you. And I'm here to see what we can do to help.

President Bush: Thank you, sir.

We'll take a few questions.

Q: Mr President—

President Bush: You're after the retirement lady. (Laughter.)

Ms. Charles: I'm now the retirement lady, I feel very old. (Laughter.)

President Bush: Well, once you leave the White House we view it as retirement. But go ahead. (Laughter.)

Ms. Charles: What's your reaction to the Saudis' announcement that we can—that the U.S. can use air bases? And also, do you feel the military deployment is adequate, do you feel comfortable with where it is?

President Bush: Well, first, we will not be discussing any of the—our military plans. It is very important for the American people to know that any public discussion of military or intelligence matters could jeopardize any mission that we may be thinking about.

Secondly, that I am most pleased with the cooperation we're getting in the Middle East. Clearly, the cooperation with our friend, the Jordanians, is strong and powerful, and we're united. But the Saudis, as well. Not only are they helping stabilize Pakistan, which is a very important part of our diplomatic efforts, they are also cooperating with us in terms of any military planning we might be doing. And I'm really pleased.

I had very good discussions—I know the King has, as well—with our Saudi Arabian friends.

Ron.

Q: Mr President, thank you. Have you had any chance to study the long and difficult conflict that the Russians had in Afghanistan? And if so, what, if anything, did you learn that might be helpful in the conflict you have coming ahead?

President Bush: Well, one of the things we will do is enforce the doctrine, part of the doctrine that says, if you harbor a terrorist, you're just as guilty as a terrorist. And in my speech to the nation I laid out the conditions that we expect the current government of Afghanistan to follow.

I am fully aware of the difficulties the Russians had in Afghanistan. Our intelligence people and our State Department people are also fully aware. It is very hard to fight a conventional war—a guerrilla war with conventional forces. And we understand that. That's why I have explained to the American people that the new war on terror is going to be a different war. It will be fought on a variety of fronts. It will be fought on a financial front; it will require the best of intelligence and the sharing of intelligence. There may or may not be a conventional component to it.

I said loud and clear, sometimes people will be able to see what we do on the television screens. Other times the American people won't be able to see what we're doing. But make no mistake about it; we're in hot pursuit. We're going to enforce the doctrine. We're going to be diligent and patient and determined to bring people to justice and to rout out terrorist activity around the world.

And so there have been lessons learned in the past, and our government is very aware of those lessons.

Jim.

Q: Mr President, if I may, for Your Highness—how difficult is it for Middle Eastern nations to unite against someone who claims to be speaking and acting on behalf of Islam?

And, Mr. President, what's your reaction to word today that the Taliban says it has now located Osama bin Laden and has delivered an invitation to him to leave the country?

President Bush: First of all—I'll answer first, and then Your Majesty. First, there is no negotiations with the Taliban. They heard what I said. And now they can act. And it's not just Mr. bin Laden that we expect to see and brought to justice; it's everybody associated with his organization that's in Afghanistan. And not only those directly associated with Mr. bin Laden, any terrorist that is housed and fed in Afghanistan needs to be handed over. And finally, we expect there to be complete destruction of terrorist camps.

That's what I told them; that's what I mean. And we expect them—we expect them to not only hear what I say, but to do something about it.

And I want to tell His Majesty what I said the other day—and then he can respond to your question. The al Qaeda people don't represent Islam, as far as America is concerned. They represent evil. They're evil people. And that's not the Muslim faith that I know and understand, nor is it the Muslim faith of millions of Americans who are proud and devout Muslims.

King Abdullah: Well, sir, as the President so well put it, what these people stand for is completely against all the principles that Arab Muslims believe in. And so, on those principles alone, I think it will be very, very easy for people to stand together. As the President said, this is a fight against evil, and the majority of Arabs and Muslims will ban together with our colleagues all over the world to be able to put an end to this horrible scourge of international terrorism. And you'll see a united front.

Mr. Johndroe: Thank you all very much.

9 President Richard Nixon's address in which he announced his intention to resign is reprinted below. The speech was delivered on Aug. 8, 1974, at 9:01 p.m. in the Oval Office at the White House. (a) Underline the statements that are most worthy of direct quotation. Defend your selections. (b) Circle statements that you would use as indirect quotations or paraphrases in a story. Defend your selections. (c) Rewrite the president's statements that you circled for exercise *b* as indirect quotations or paraphrases.

Good evening:

This is the 37th time I have spoken to you from this office, where so many decisions have been made that shaped the history of this nation. Each time I have done so to discuss with you some matter that I believe affected the national interest.

In all the decisions I have made in my public life, I have always tried to do what was best for the Nation. Throughout the long and difficult period of Watergate, I have felt it was my duty to persevere, to make every possible effort to complete the term of office to which you elected me.

In the past few days, however, it has become evident to me that I no longer have a strong enough political base in the Congress to justify continuing that effort. As long as there was such a base, I felt strongly that it was necessary to see the constitutional process through to its conclusion, that to do otherwise would be unfaithful to the spirit of that deliberately difficult process and a dangerously destabilizing precedent for the future.

But with the disappearance of that base, I now believe that the constitutional purpose has been served, and there is no longer a need for the process to be prolonged.

I would have preferred to carry through to the finish whatever the personal agony it would have involved, and my family unanimously urged me to do so. But the interest of the Nation must always come before any personal considerations.

From the discussions I have had with Congressional and other leaders, I have concluded that because of the Watergate matter I might not have the support of the Congress that I would consider necessary to back the very difficult decisions and carry out the duties of this office in the way the interests of the Nation would require.

I have never been a quitter. To leave office before my term is completed is abhorrent to every instinct in my body. But as President, I must put the interest of America first. America needs a full-time President and a full-time Congress, particularly at this time with problems we face at home and abroad.

To continue to fight through the months ahead for my personal vindication would almost totally absorb the time and attention of both the President and the Congress in a period when our entire focus should be on the great issues of peace abroad and prosperity without inflation at home.

Therefore, I shall resign the Presidency effective at noon tomorrow. Vice President Ford will be sworn in as President at that hour in this office.

As I recall the high hopes for America with which we began this second term, I feel a great sadness that I will not be here in this office working on your behalf to achieve those hopes in the next 2½ years. But in turning over direction of the Government to Vice President Ford, I know, as I told the Nation when I nominated him for that office 10 months ago, that the leadership of America will be in good hands.

In passing this office to the Vice President, I also do so with the profound sense of the weight of responsibility that will fall on his shoulders tomorrow and, therefore, of the understanding, the patience, the cooperation he will need from all Americans.

As he assumes that responsibility, he will deserve the help and the support of all of us. As we look to the future, the first essential is to begin healing the wounds of this Nation, to put the bitterness and divisions of the recent past behind us, and to rediscover those shared ideals that lie at the heart of our strength and unity as a great and as a free people.

By taking this action, I hope that I will have hastened the start of the process of healing which is so desperately needed in America.

I regret deeply any injuries that may have been done in the course of the events that led to this decision. I would say only that if some of my judgments were wrong, and some were wrong, they were made in what I believed at the time to be the best interest of the Nation.

To those who have stood with me during these past difficult months, to my family, my friends, to many others who joined in supporting my cause because they believed it was right, I will be eternally grateful for your support.

And to those who have not felt able to give me your support, let me say I leave with no bitterness toward those who have opposed me, because all of us, in the final analysis, have been concerned with the good of the country, however our judgments might differ.

So, let us all now join together in affirming that common commitment and in helping our new President succeed for the benefit of all Americans.

I shall leave this office with regret at not completing my term, but with gratitude for the privilege of serving as your President for the past 5½ years. These years have been a momentous time in the history of our Nation and the world. They have been a time of achievement in which we can all be proud, achievements that represent the shared efforts of the Administration, the Congress, and the people.

But the challenges ahead are equally great, and they, too, will require the support and the efforts of the Congress and the people working in cooperation with the new Administration.

We have ended America's longest war, but in the work of securing a lasting peace in the world, the goals ahead are even more far-reaching and more difficult. We must complete a structure of peace so that it will be said of this generation, our generation of Americans, by the people of all nations, not only that we ended one war but that we prevented future wars.

We have unlocked the doors that for a quarter of a century stood between the United States and the People's Republic of China.

We must now ensure that the one quarter of the world's people who live in the People's Republic of China will be and remain not our enemies but our friends.

In the Middle East, 100 million people in the Arab countries, many of whom have considered us their enemy for nearly 20 years, now look on us as their friends. We must continue to build on that friendship so that peace can settle at last over the Middle East and so that the cradle of civilization will not become its grave.

Together with the Soviet Union we have made the crucial breakthroughs that have begun the process of limiting nuclear arms. But we must set as our goal not just limiting but reducing and finally destroying these terrible weapons so that they cannot destroy civilization and so that the threat of nuclear war will no longer hang over the world and the people.

We have opened a new relation with the Soviet Union. We must continue to develop and expand that new relationship so that the two strongest nations of the world will live together in cooperation rather than confrontation.

Around the world, in Asia, in Africa, in Latin America, in the Middle East, there are millions of people who live in terrible poverty, even starvation. We must keep as our goal turning away from production for war and expanding production for peace so that people everywhere on this earth can at last look forward in their children's time, if not in our own time, to having the necessities for a decent life.

Here in America, we are fortunate that most of our people have not only the blessings of liberty but also the means to live full and good and, by the world's standards, even abundant lives. We must press on, however, toward a goal of not only more and better jobs but of full opportunity for every American and of what we are striving so hard right now to achieve, prosperity without inflation.

For more than a quarter of a century in

public life I have shared in the turbulent history of this era. I have fought for what I believed in. I have tried to the best of my ability to discharge those duties and meet those responsibilities that were entrusted to me.

Sometimes I have succeeded and sometimes I have failed, but always I have taken heart from what Theodore Roosevelt once said about the man in the arena, "whose face is marred by dust and sweat and blood, who strives valiantly, who errs and comes short again and again because there is not effort without error and shortcoming, but who does actually strive to do the deed, who knows the great enthusiasms, the great devotions, who spends himself in a worthy cause, who at the best knows in the end the triumphs of high achievements and who at the worst, if he fails, at least fails while daring greatly."

I pledge to you tonight that as long as I have a breath of life in my body, I shall continue in that spirit. I shall continue to work for the great causes to which I have been dedicated throughout my years as a Congressman, a Senator, a Vice President, and President, the cause of peace not just for America but among all nations, prosperity, justice, and opportunity for all of our people.

There is one cause above all to which I have been devoted and to which I shall always be devoted for as long as I live.

When I first took the oath of office as President 5½ years ago, I made this sacred commitment, to "consecrate my office, my energies, and all the wisdom I can summon to the cause of peace among nations."

I have done my very best in all the days since to be true to that pledge. As a result of these efforts, I am confident that the world is a safer place today, not only for the people of America but for the people of all nations, and that all of our children have a better chance than before of living in peace rather than dying in war.

This, more than anything, is what I hoped to achieve when I sought the Presidency. This, more than anything, is what I hope will be my legacy to you, to our country, as I leave the Presidency.

To have served in this office is to have felt a very personal sense of kinship with each and every American. In leaving it, I do so with this prayer: May God's grace be with you in all the days ahead.

9

Features

Review Questions

1 What are the major differences between a hard news story and a feature?

2 Explain "immediate news value."

3 What is "Jell-O journalism"?

4 What is a personality profile? Give an example.

5 What is a human interest story? Give an example.

6 What is a trend story? Give an example.

7 What is an in-depth story? Give an example.

8 What is a backgrounder? Give an example.

9 What steps does a writer typically follow when organizing a feature?

10 What four factors does a writer use to determine the theme of a feature?

a

b

c

d

11 What is voice? Give an example.

12 Why is dialogue an important component of feature writing?

Suggested Exercises

1 Here are the opening nine paragraphs of a hard news story in *The East Valley Tribune* in suburban Phoenix, reporting that the city's elementary school district approved a new contract for teachers. Rewrite the story into a feature. What interviews might you conduct, or what additional sources might you consult to rewrite it? You can assume that by the time your feature runs, the news has been reported.

Tempe Elementary District teacher and governing board bargaining teams agreed Thursday to a two-year teacher salary, benefits and working conditions package.

The plan calls for a 2.65 percent increase in the teacher base salary next school year and a 4.5 percent base increase the following year, if voters approve a budget override.

The package will not become policy until a majority of the board and teachers approve it.

Connie Thomas, Getz School principal and board team spokeswoman, said the board would offer a 2.65 percent base increase as a compromise between its earlier 2 percent proposal and the teachers' 3.3 percent proposal.

"The board feels that that's its absolute last offer, 2.65, because nothing beyond that is possible," Thomas said.

Teachers will also receive a traditional 5 percent longevity increase and a 4.25 percent education increase for eligible teachers with extra college credits.

Starting salary for the next school year will be $17,470, if the package is approved.

Starting salary for the second year of the contract would be $18,256. Base salary this year is $17,019.

The plan calls for a top teacher salary next school year of $37,624.

2 Clip from a newspaper a feature story, and analyze it. What type of lead is used? What is the thread? What is the theme of the story? Mark the transitions. Circle sentences in which the writer used voice. Is dialogue used? Is the story a personality profile, a human interest story, a trend story, an in-depth or a backgrounder?

3 Use the following Associated Press story to write a feature about the link between smoking and drinking. The story deals with a psychiatrist at the University of Vermont who believes that people who give up smoking could improve the chances of fighting their alcoholism. Find local sources who can talk about the subject. Try to begin your feature with a lead block, perhaps built around a local expert or someone who successfully fought cigarette and alcohol addictions.

Smoking and drinking: Statistics show that people who have one addiction often have the other.

Many alcoholics who have stopped drinking hesitate to tackle their smoking habit, believing the added stress could hurt their chances of staying sober.

A University of Vermont psychiatrist, however, believes that people who give up smoking could improve the chances of fighting their alcoholism.

"It's a myth that stopping (smoking) will make you relapse," said Dr. John Hughes, a professor at University of Vermont's College of Medicine who has been studying smokers and their efforts to quit for 20 years. "We've got the scientific evidence that shows this is not true."

For a study funded by the National Institute of Alcohol and Alcohol Abuse, Hughes is recruiting volunteers from the Burlington area who have successfully battled alcoholism and now want freedom from smoking. He hopes his research will uncover new ways of helping recovering alcoholics give up cigarettes, too.

Studies show people who smoke are more likely to have drinking problems, Hughes said. In the population at large, the likelihood is 7 percent. Among people who have never smoked, it's .2 percent. For heavy smokers, the probability is 18 percent.

Nobody knows why drinking and smoking so frequently go together, but most doctors agree they do.

"Almost all alcoholics are smokers," said Dr. Neil Benowitz, an internal medicine professor at the University of California in San Francisco who has studied nicotine addiction. "But there's been very little systematic research of how to treat someone who has both diagnoses."

Alcohol is a depressant and smoking is a stimulant; one might be used to balance the effects of the other, Hughes said. Studies on animals show smoking can mitigate some of drinking's negative effects, like nausea or sedation.

"So smoking may allow people to drink more," Hughes said.

With his study, which is being carried out concurrently at the University of Minnesota at Minneapolis, Hughes hopes to replicate findings that he stumbled upon during earlier research on nicotine substitutes.

In that study, some subjects were given a nicotine patch and some were given a placebo. The patch helped both drinkers and nondrinkers to quit smoking more than the placebo did. What interested Hughes was the placebo's effect: None of the recovering alcoholics given the placebo managed to quit smoking.

"They found that smokers that did have a history of alcohol dependency were much more dependent on nicotine," Hughes said of that study. But the stress of quitting smoking didn't necessarily harm their sobriety; "none went back to drinking," he said.

In the current study, 75 recovering alcoholics will receive group behavior therapy and counseling to help them quit smoking. Then the earlier study will be repeated: Half the group will receive a nicotine substitute, and half a placebo.

"Now we want to know: Do they have more physical withdrawal symptoms?" Hughes said. The study will also shed more light on whether quitting smoking does threaten sobriety. Hughes thinks giving up cigarettes might actually help recovering alcoholics stay sober. "When people stop drinking or stop smoking, many times it's part of an overall life change," he said.

Research on the connections between nicotine and alcoholics is badly needed, said Dr. Jack Henningfield, a researcher in drug addiction at the National Institutes of Health.

"The sad thing is that this population just hasn't been studied much," Henningfield said. "That's sad because the chances are a lot of those people may kick their so-called primary drug and die a miserable tobacco-related death."

Vermont funds cocaine and alcohol abuse hotlines and helps support treatment programs for many different types of addictions. But there is no state support for fighting smoking, Hughes said, because tobacco doesn't appear as dangerous to society as other drugs. But it should, he said.

"These (smokers) who have worked all their lives ... when it's time for retirement, they come down with heart attack or emphysema," Hughes said. "That's the tragic part."

Part Three

Gathering Information

10

Interviewing

Review Questions

1 What are the three stages in an interview? Explain the importance of each stage.

2 A reporter has an appointment to interview a famous author, who is coming to town to promote her new book. What steps should the reporter follow before the interview?

3 What are the steps to follow in setting up an interview?

4 Explain the difference between funnel and inverted-funnel interviews.

5 What is a closed-ended question? Give two examples.

6 What is an open-ended question? Give two examples.

7 What are the guidelines a reporter can follow when asking a personal question?

8 Why are follow-up questions important during an interview?

9 How does a reporter go about establishing rapport with a source?

10 What are the guidelines a reporter can follow to persuade sources to go on the record or not to become hostile?

11 Why are observations important during an interview? What are some of the things a reporter should observe? Give two examples of observation from newspaper stories.

12 Discuss the advantages and disadvantages of using a tape recorder in an interview.

13 Where should a reporter place his or her note pad during an interview?

14 What are the advantages and disadvantages of telephone interviewing? What are the guidelines to follow when conducting an interview over the telephone?

15 Discuss the advantages and disadvantages of conducting an interview via e-mail.

16 What should a reporter do when the interview has ended?

Suggested Exercises

1 Denise Franklin, a reporter at the *Santa Cruz* (Calif.) *Sentinel,* interviewed a licensed family, marriage and child therapist for a story on being single. Her story concentrated on a workshop that the therapist, Paula Rotman, holds for single people as well as Rotman's advice on building relationships. Use the following information—Franklin's notes (below) and a flier announcing the workshop (next page)—to construct a story based on one interview. The notes you are given for the story are exactly as Franklin took them, except that her abbreviations are spelled out to make it easier for you. The direct quotations are marked; the rest of the material can be paraphrased.

Paula Rotman

In fall, will become a 2-day class.

A lot of those who come to workshop are newly divorced, newly widowed or in a stuck place in their lives.

Usually ½ men, ½ women and mix of single, divorced, widowed and a mix of ages attend the workshops.

They are either looking for someone or want skills to let go of the ended relationship. They want a way to let go and really use their energy for the future, for themselves and future relationships.

Many have dated as teens, married for many years and then they are single. "They don't have the social skills and the knowledge of what's going on out there. There has been a social and sexual revolution."

"Their questions are as simple as when out on a date, who pays? to as complex as what's right for me—an affair, living together or marriage? What is it I want from this relationship?"

Her advice: "Make choices that are comfortable for you. In your sexuality, are you a monogamous person who'd like to remarry or would you like to date several people and have many relationships?"

The most common complaint: Where to meet and how to meet. "A lot of people seem to meet in my class. It seems to be a good safe place to meet people in a non-threatening atmosphere."

She suggests "Do something you really enjoy doing, out of your interest, not out of your loneliness."

For example, she plays tennis and "if I meet someone playing tennis, I'm going to be a much more interesting person because I'm there to enjoy myself, not because I'm lonely."

She's single and a single parent. She's in private practice in Capitola and teaches at Cabrillo in women's studies, as well as workshops.

What's exciting about the workshop is they get to see their commonality. "They both want love and companionship and are afraid of reaching out."

"One of the biggest things that most women bring up is they get into self-defeating patterns, picking the wrong person or type of person. The first thing you do is see that you have a pattern and it's not working for you. An option is to date a wide variety of people to see how you feel with different types of people. You get them to date you by working on your self-esteem, which we work on in the workshop. We perform specific exercises to help us like ourselves better and to accept compliments when someone strokes us."

How to keep from appearing hungry? "Satisfy that need for intimacy with other friendships or relatives so that you don't feel so hungry for intimacy."

When do singles go wrong? "We put too much stress on the love relationship, as what is going to satisfy us the most. The stress should be put on enjoyment of our work, our friends, our interests, our spiritual life. We have to realize that a love relationship will only be one part of our whole life and we'll eventually find it. And we must believe that nothing lasts forever. Either through death or divorce, some of us are going to be alone at some time, so we need to know how to put together a

Cabrillo College

COMMUNITY EDUCATION
PRESENTS

BUILDING RELATIONSHIPS
STARTING OVER

ARE YOU A SINGLE, DIVORCED OR WIDOWED MAN OR WOMAN INTERESTED IN ENHANCING YOUR SOCIAL SKILLS?

THIS WORKSHOP, FACILITATED BY PAULA ROTMAN, M.S., A LICENSED MARRIAGE, FAMILY, AND CHILD THERAPIST, WILL START YOU ON YOUR WAY TOWARD MORE FULFILLING RELATIONSHIPS.

TOPICS INCLUDE:

- **SELF-ESTEEM**
- **DATING AND SEXUALITY**
- **COMMUNICATION SKILLS**

DATE: SAT., MAY 3

TIME: 10 A.M. - 4 P.M.

PLACE: CABRILLO ROOM 406

FEE: $35

Could enroll day of class

REGISTRATION AND INFORMATION
CABRILLO COLLEGE SESNON HOUSE
479-6331/688-6466

successful life."

If you think finding Mr. or Mrs. Right will solve all your problems "it will put too much stress on a relationship and it will never work."

Singles are really concerned about their sexuality. "They want to know how to handle children when they are dating." Constant question is what to do about the children when you want to have a special person spend the night. That has come up for the 10 years she's been giving the workshop.

She tells them: Do what you feel comfortable with. "And I tell them: Number one, children know everything. They think they can hide things from the children, but they can't. What can the adult comfortably handle? The difference is whether you show the children a committed relationship or many different partners. You are showing them two different things."

Also deal with age, past relationships, anger and hurt. "In widowhood, there can be a lot of anger that the person left you. Widowed people don't always realize what they are doing to themselves. In the workshop we get them to talk to others about it, so their energy isn't used in a negative way."

"Look at a new man, new woman, people who are liberated. Women are out in the workplace earning money and there are men who want to be more sensitive and feeling."

"Many people have been in traditional marriages and they now want relationships that are more liberated and more equal and they want to learn how to do that."

She asks people to ask themselves where they are on a traditional-egalitarian relationships scale. It is really tricky. People are working out the details. These egalitarian relationships are very new. "A lot of men in the workshop who had a traditional relationship said they no longer want to be the main money earner and the emotional bearer of the relationship. Take a couple who both want an egalitarian relationship but whose models were their parents or their first marriage. He sometimes wants to have dinner made for him and have the house clean when he gets home from work; she sometimes wants him to be the provider so she can stay home and raise the baby."

Most people are eventually looking for committed relationships.

"People are afraid of making the same mistake twice. The more they learn about themselves and past relationships, the less chance of that happening."

"I know people who have met that way. People who've married through an ad in a magazine. Just be careful. Meet here first in broad daylight where others are around."

"The other thing is, if you want to meet someone, you've got to get out there. Everyone would like to meet through friends or relatives, but it doesn't always happen that way. You've got to enlarge your world. That's the hard part. We work on that too. We do role playing. How to meet in certain situations."

She teaches the workshop "because it is fun and the class is fun. Nobody is doing things like that and it is so important. I don't know why people aren't doing groups anymore. Groups are out, but they are needed."

Relationships take time and energy. That's the thing that makes many marriages go under. "Successful singlehood is better than a bad marriage. Most people would rather be in a committed relationship, but if it is a bad one, you're better off alone. And how do they know when it's time to go?"

2 The White House press secretary meets with reporters in the briefing room nearly every day to talk about the latest and most compelling issues facing the president. The press secretary also answers questions from reporters. Your assignment is to go into the White House home page on the World Wide Web (*http://www.whitehouse.gov/news/briefings*) and read the latest press briefing. Write a news story as though you were the sole reporter listening to the press secretary and then asking the questions. Assume that you conducted the interview this morning and are writing the story for print later today.

11

Computer-Assisted Reporting and Research

Review Questions

1 Define the following.

a CAR

b World Wide Web

c Internet

d Web browser

e Search engine

f Listserv

g Usenet news group

h Primary sources

i Secondary sources

j URL

k HTML

l e-mail

m Moderated listserv

n Bookmark

2 What book started the computer-assisted reporting movement? Who was the author?

3 Name a Website for:

a A directory of Web sites

b Free e-mail

c A directory of e-mail listservs

d An archive of newsgroup messages

e A Web index generated by spider/robot software

f A metasearch database

4 What is the likely URL for:

a Ford Motor Co.

b Arizona State University

c The Audobon Society

d United States Marine Corps

5 What type of organization would use each of these domain name suffixes?

a .com

b .org

c .edu

d .mil

e .net

6 What are the five criteria for evaluating a web page?

a

b

c

d

e

Suggested Exercises

1 Visit the White House Website (*www.whitehouse.gov*). Go to the Briefing Room and find a recent speech by the president. Use it to write a news story about the speech.

2 Use Dejanews (*www.dejanews.com*) to search for newsgroups where the disease Hepatitis C is discussed. Read enough of the messages to prepare a list of questions you might ask of someone who has the disease if you were doing a story about it.

3 Use L-Soft (*www.lsoft.com/lists*) or Tile.net (*www.tile.net*) to find a journalism-related e-mail listserv or another topic of interest to you. Subscribe to the list.

4 Use one of the Web search engines to find background about these people, places or things:

a Brant Houston

b The Drake Equation

c Tortola

d Larry Burrows

e Thalassemia

5 Search the Web for an online version of the Central Intelligence Agency's "World Factbook." Use it to find the major exports of the country of Belize.

6 Go to the Federal Bureau of Investigation's Web site. In the Crime Statistics section, find out how many murders were reported in the Uniform Crime Report for the most recent year for a city near you.

7 Find the online site of your local or hometown newspaper. (Search the *Editor & Publisher* site at *www.mediainfo.com/emedia.*) Does the site take advantage of multimedia capabilities, such as using sound or video? Is there a searchable archive of past stories? Does the site offer large databases that couldn't be printed in the paper, such as crime listings by neighborhood, detailed school test score data or property assessments by street? What else is good—and bad—about the site?

12

Surveys

Review Questions

1 Define the following terms.

a Precision journalism

b Focal question

c Random selection

d Population

e Skip interval

f Sample

g Sampling error

h Frequency distribution

2 Discuss the pros and cons of newspapers' use of survey methods to gather information for stories.

3 Discuss the strategy of forming mostly closed-ended questions for surveys.

4 Discuss why it is good to include some open-ended questions in surveys.

5 Discuss why you should always test survey questions before conducting the survey.

6 Discuss the advantages and disadvantages of the following methods of gathering information.

a Face-to-face interview

b Mailed questionnaire

c Telephone interview

7 The chapter notes that the first consideration when writing a story based on a survey is to analyze the data carefully before starting to write. Writers should ask themselves: What findings would be of most interest to the audience? List other suggestions to consider when writing stories based on survey research.

8 List and discuss the guidelines suggested by the National Council on Public Polling for writing stories based on survey research.

9 List and discuss the 10 factors that can distort the outcome of polls, as compiled by James Simon.

a

b

c

d

e

f

g

h

i

j

Suggested Exercises

Students in the mass communication research class and the advanced reporting class at the University of North Carolina at Chapel Hill combine their efforts each year to produce and report a survey called The Carolina Poll. Many people profit: students in the research class have an opportunity to apply the theory they study; students in the reporting class have a chance to base their stories on fresh, relevant, computer-generated data; newspapers in the state that cannot afford to commission or conduct a statewide poll receive stories from the UNC News Bureau to publish; and readers in North Carolina are enlightened about contemporary issues. The exercises in this section are based on stories written at and distributed by the University of North Carolina at Chapel Hill.

1 Before digesting the statistical information and writing stories based on it, read the following story, which was written by Doug Hughes and distributed by the UNC News Bureau. It helps to put polls into further perspective. What is the thrust of the story?

CHAPEL HILL, N.C.—David Neal plans to vote for Walter Mondale, but no pollster will know it.

Even with all the polling that's taken place this election season in North Carolina, the political opinions of this 27-year-old Durham resident aren't going to make it into the papers or TV news.

In fact, few people like Neal—black, young, male—are represented in the polls that have become so common. But what makes Neal's exclusion almost certain is that he doesn't have a telephone.

Neal is not unique. In his neighborhood, bounded by Roxboro Street to the east and the railroad to the west, more than one household in four doesn't have telephone service, according to the 1980 U.S. Census.

About 11 percent of all North Carolina households lacked telephones in 1980, according to census figures, compared with seven percent across the country. In the counties of Bertie, Bladen, Hoke, Jones, Robeson and Swain, more than 21 percent of households had no phones in 1980.

Households without telephones present special problems to poll takers, since almost no interviewing is conducted in person. Instead, most polls are done over the phone, using statistical techniques to make the results as precise as possible.

One of the most common of these sampling techniques is random-digit dialing, in which a computer is programmed to create random telephone numbers that give each number an equal chance of being called. Nearly all telephone polls, including the Gallup, Harris and Carolina polls, develop their calling lists this way.

However, the power of sampling methods such as this is limited in neighborhoods like Neal's. Because more than a quarter of his neighbors lack phones, they are much less likely to be represented in opinion polls than residents in more affluent sections of Durham, where nearly all homes have phones.

Most polls routinely underrepresent blacks and the poor, the groups most often without phones. Those who are often away from home, younger people and men in particular, are also underrepresented. People in these underrepresented groups probably have opinions in common that aren't surveyed—meaning the opinions of whole segments of society are ignored in most polls.

Although the likelihood is high that the opinions of people like himself are not represented by the polls, Neal said he doesn't think they are inaccurate. The published polls that show [President] Reagan with a strong lead over Mondale in North Carolina are believable, he said. "People seem to like Reagan a lot," he said. "It looks like they are going to put him back in office again."

However, the former [Jimmy] Carter supporter sees himself on the losing side again. "I think Walter Mondale could do the best job, could help the people the most," Neal said.

Pollsters take note.

2 The following information is from a telephone survey conducted from Feb. 17 through March 1 by journalism and political science students at the University of North Carolina at Chapel Hill. Write a story based on the information.

Some 1,209 adults were telephoned at random in the state of North Carolina. Interviewers asked this question: "Do you think abortion should be legal under any circumstances, should be legal only under certain circumstances or should never be legal?"

The results of those who had an opinion: 19 percent said that abortion should be legal under any circumstances; 60 percent said under certain circumstances; 21 percent said that abortion should never be legal.

At the 95 percent level of confidence, the sampling error of the poll is 3 percentage points.

Professors Philip Meyer and Jane Brown supervised the poll, which is conducted two times a year by the UNC School of Journalism.

The Carolina Poll had these additional findings: 83 percent of respondents in the 18–34 age group supported legal abortion; 79 percent of the 35–54 age group supported legal abortion; 72 percent of those over age 55 supported legal abortion. Also, 85 percent of those who had at least a high school diploma supported legal abortion.

It was noted that many respondents who said that abortion should be legal under certain circumstances said that they approved of abortion only in cases of rape or to save the woman's life.

Results of other polls cited: A 1980 survey sponsored by the National Abortion Rights Action League showed that 83 percent of 1,000 Americans polled supported legal abortion. That poll's respondents were randomly chosen from voter registration lists and were asked the same question that appeared on the Carolina Poll.

A 1980 Gallup Poll asked the same question. The sample was 1,948 adults nationwide. Seventy-eight percent supported legal abortion.

3 The following information is from a telephone survey to determine whether North Carolina residents would favor a lottery to raise money for government expenses. The survey was conducted between Feb. 25 and March 3 by students at the University of North Carolina's School of Journalism and Mass Communication. Write a story based on the information.

Nearly 600 residents were telephoned at random in the poll. Interviewers asked these questions: (1) "Do you think a state lottery would be a good idea or a bad idea?" (2) "If North Carolina had a state lottery, would you participate or not?"

Results of question No. 1: 59 percent said they favored a lottery; 28 percent said they opposed the idea; 13 percent said they had no opinion.

Results of question No. 2: 55 percent said they would participate (61 percent of the males polled said they would participate; 50 percent of the females said they would; 66 percent of single people said they would; 55 percent of married people said they would; 67 percent among those under age 40 said they would; 54 percent of those in their 40s said they would; 34 percent of those over 60 said they would; 60 percent of those with incomes above $10,000 said they would; 43 percent of those with incomes below $10,000 said they would).

Also: The poll showed that the level of participation would go up with education level.

Supporters of the legislation said that it could generate $100 million a year for the state's general fund.

Quotations:

Rep. Jeanne Fenner, D-Wilson, who introduced the lottery bill in the House: "It's a misconception that this is going to take food off the table of the poor. It's not true. If it's not bearing out in other states, why should it happen in North Carolina?"

Sen. Richard Barnes, D-Forsyth, who introduced the measure in the Senate, responded to the charge that past lotteries had come under attack because they were fraudulently run: "We've moved forward in progress with lotteries."

The state of North Carolina had 107 lotteries between 1759 and 1834. Funds were used to construct schools, including the main University of North Carolina at Chapel Hill administration building, manufacturing plants and churches.

The measure has its critics.

The Rev. Coy Privette of Kannapolis, president of the state's Christian Action League, said: "The state, of all people, wants to exploit the weakness of its citizens."

Privette said in a telephone interview that he opposed the lottery because, in addition to the moral issue, it encourages corruption and unfairly taxes the poor. He said: "It seeks to seduce money away from those who are least able to pay."

Privette continued: "They [lotteries] were doomed as failures in the 17th and 18th centuries. So now we're coming right around and adopting something that is bound to fail."

George Yamin, public relations director for the New York State Lottery, where about half of the adult residents participate, was quoted. He said that the average ticket buyer there is 45 years old, white, male and earns more than $20,000 a year.

Privette called attention to Gov. James B. Hunt's opposition to the plan. Privette said: "It's hard to get anything through the General Assembly if the governor is against it."

Privette also said that the Christian Action League would work against the measure in the legislature.

Privette discounted the poll results. He said that actual voting behavior would be "a totally different ball game," and he predicted defeat for a lottery referendum.

At the 95 percent level of confidence, the sampling error of the poll is 4 percentage points.

4 The following information is from a telephone survey conducted from Oct. 11–15 by students at the University of North Carolina's School of Journalism and Mass Communication. Write a story based on the information.

The poll asked 598 adult North Carolinians this question: "Do you think children who have been diagnosed as having AIDS should be allowed to attend school with other children?"

Margin of error in the Carolina Poll is 4 percentage points. This means that in 19 of 20 samples of this type, the results would vary by no more than 4 percent from what would have been obtained if every telephone in the state had been dialed.

Telephone numbers dialed were chosen by a random computer process by KPC Research, which is the market research arm of Knight Publishing Co., in Charlotte.

Sponsors of the poll were the School of Journalism and the Institute for Research in Social Science at the University of North Carolina at Chapel Hill.

Results: 64 percent said AIDS children should be allowed to attend school; 23 percent said they should not; 13 percent said they had no opinion.

Of the high school dropouts who responded to the survey, 54 percent said they would allow AIDS children to attend school with healthy children; 68 percent of those with a college education said they would allow it.

Quotations from Kathy Kerr, a health educator with the AIDS Control Program of the North Carolina Division of Health Services: "It's encouraging to have more than half say they would (let AIDS children attend classes with other children). I think a few years ago in this epidemic there was a lot more AIDS hysteria and probably a lot more people said they wouldn't let AIDS children attend school with other children.

"More and more people are recognizing that AIDS is not transmitted casually. You certainly don't get AIDS by sitting next to someone in class."

5 The following information is from a telephone survey conducted from Oct. 11–15 by journalism students at the University of North Carolina. Write a story based on the information.

Telephone numbers were chosen by a random computer process by KPC Research, the market research arm of Knight Publishing Co., in Charlotte. The poll was sponsored by the School of Journalism and the Institute for Research in Social Science at UNC.

Some 598 adult residents of North

Carolina agreed to be interviewed by telephone. Sampling error is 4 percentage points. In other words, in 100 samples of this size, 95 would yield results varying by no more than 4 percent from what would have been obtained if every telephone in the state had been dialed.

The question that was posed: "Would you say that you are very happy, pretty happy or not too happy?"

Overall results: 31 percent said they were very happy; 55 percent said they were pretty happy; 14 percent said they were not too happy. The results are similar to current national surveys.

Some additional breakdowns:

Of residents of North Carolina who make at least $30,000 each year, 39 percent are very happy; 25 percent of those who make less than $30,000 are very happy.

Of college graduates and persons with less than an eighth grade education, 34 percent said they are very happy; 21 percent of high school dropouts and 28 percent of the respondents with some college education said they were very happy. Dr. Arne L. Kalleberg, professor of sociology at UNC, was asked what might account for the differences based on education. She said that persons who dropped out of high school and persons with some college who did not finish might have expected good jobs that did not materialize. Conversely, persons with less than an eighth grade education did not expect great jobs or a lot of money, thus making for a happier group.

More breakdowns:

Of married respondents, 34 percent said they are very happy; 26 percent of those who are separated or not married said they are very happy.

Of those respondents under age 25, 33 percent said they are very happy; 27 percent of those over age 60 said they are very happy.

Of blacks who responded, 25 percent said they are not too happy; 11 percent of whites said they are not too happy. Of Republicans, 38 percent said they are very happy; 35 percent of Independents said they are very happy; 27 percent of Democrats said they are very happy.

Of nonfrequent readers of newspapers, 21 percent said they are not too happy; 11 percent of frequent newspaper readers said they are not too happy.

6 The following information is from a telephone survey conducted from Oct. 11–15 by journalism students at the University of North Carolina. Write a story based on the information.

The survey asked 598 adult residents of North Carolina to judge their altruistic qualities.

The questions: "How willing would you be to do something for the good of your community even if this was not in your own best interest—extremely willing, very willing, somewhat or not very willing? How often do you go out of your way to be courteous or kind to strangers—very often, sometimes, rarely or never?"

Results: 58 percent said they would be only somewhat willing or not very willing at all to do good for their neighbors if not in their own best interests. Some 38 percent said they would be extremely willing or very willing to help their community.

When asked how often they go out of their way to be courteous to strangers, 91 percent said they go out of their way at least some of the time. About 9 percent said they rarely or never were kind to strangers.

Dr. Bibb Latane, professor of psychology at UNC and a leading altruism researcher, was questioned about the results. He said he found them to be surprising.

Latane quotation: "There is a big difference in what people say they will do and what they will really do when a situation arises. The data have a lot to do with impression management—not with a measure of actual helpfulness."

Impression management is what people believe they will do, not what action they really perform in a given situation.

Latane quotation: "Their actual behavior is not predictable."

Margin of error of the survey is 4 percentage points. This means that in 95 out of 100 samples of this type, the results would vary by no more than 4 percent from what would have been obtained if every telephone in North Carolina had been dialed.

The poll was sponsored by the School of Journalism at UNC and the Institute for Research in Social Science. Phone numbers were chosen by a random computer process by KPC Research, the market research arm of Knight Publishing Co., in Charlotte.

Other results: More than 92 percent of white respondents said they were courteous to strangers; 87 percent of minorities said they were. Almost 40 percent of the Democrats and Independents said they would be willing to do good for their community regardless of personal benefits. Some 33 percent of the Republicans said they would be. Sex and race did not produce significant results on altruistic behaviors toward the community.

Part Four

Basic Assignments

13

Obituaries

Review Questions

1 What is the philosophy of most newspapers concerning the publication of obituaries?

2 Some newspapers strive to expand their obituaries beyond basic information, such as age, memberships, survivors and service details. What are some of the strategies and approaches that reporters use to write obituaries that provide more than just basic facts?

3 Discuss general newspaper obit policies on:

a Names, nicknames and courtesy titles

b Ages

c Addresses

d Causes of death

e Suicide

f Handling sensitive information, such as a criminal record

g Flowers and memorials

4 List some basic sources for obituary information.

5 Accuracy, of course, is the building block of good journalism; it is particularly important when writing obituaries. What steps can reporters take to ensure that information in obits is correct?

6 A fear at every newspaper is to publish or air an obituary that is a hoax. How can reporters guard against this?

7 Discuss the difference between same-day and second-day obits.

Suggested Exercises

1 Prepare advance obits for the following (list sources you consulted).

a President of the United States

b U.S. senator from your state

c Governor of your state

d Mayor of your community

e President of your university or college

f Superintendent of public schools in your community

g Publisher of your local daily newspaper

2 Write a same-day obit based on the following information, which is from *The Evansville* (Ind.) *Press.*

Name—Lois Bray

Age—68

Address—3017 Sheridan Road, Evansville

Died—at 5:05 a.m. today

Where—Welborn Baptist Hospital

Background—member of St. Paul United Church of Christ on Big Cynthiana Road; was well known as an interior designer in the Tri-State area, where she had worked for a long time; most recently had been employed at the Design Boutique on Lincoln Avenue

Quotation—"She was a talented person," said Jane Hayden, one of the owners of Design Boutique. "She was a very congenial, loving person."

Preceded in death—by her husband, Clarence Wilbur Bray. He died in 1982.

Survivors—son, Robert Bray of Norfolk, W.Va.; a grandson, Rob Bray, Norfolk, W.Va.; and a brother, Francis Blake of Alabama

Services—pending at Alexander Funeral Home North Chapel

3 Write a second-day obit based on the information in exercise 2. Assume, however, that the funeral services will be at 10 a.m. Friday in the St. Paul United Church of Christ, Big Cynthiana Road.

4 Write an obit based on the following information.

Name—John J. Johnson

Date of death—Monday

Age—74

Address—1111 Main St., Riverdale

Occupation—president, Farmer's Bank, Riverdale

Cause of death—heart attack suffered during first quarter of Monday night's Riverdale High School basketball game against Geneva

Date of services—Thursday

Time—11 a.m.

Place—McGrew-Jones Funeral Home, 2121 Central Ave., Riverdale

Background—President of state bankers' association in 1977; member of the Riverdale school board, 1960–1970; member of the Riverdale City Council, 1970–1978; earned M.B.A. degree from Riverdale University in 1950

Survivors—wife, Helen

Burial—Evergreen Cemetery

Memorials—local heart association

Additional background from newspaper clippings found in morgue—played basketball for Riverdale University, where he was an all-conference performer; was born and reared in Riverdale; was convicted in 1944 for draft evasion and served six months in prison; his father was a longtime minister of the First Presbyterian Church of Riverdale.

5 Write an obit based on the following information, which is from an Associated Press story.

Name—Dave Thomas

Date of death—Tuesday around midnight at his home in Fort Lauderdale, Fla.

Age—69

Cause of death—Liver cancer. (He had been undergoing kidney dialysis and had earlier undergone quadruple heart bypass surgery.)

Background—He was the founder and senior chairman of Wendy's International, one of the world's most successful fast-food enterprises. Wendy's became a household name when he began pitching his burgers and fries in television commercials in 1989. He always wore a white short-sleeved shirt and red tie. He made more than 800 humorous ads, sometimes featuring stars such as bluesman B. B. King and soap opera queen Susan Lucci. His homespun ads contributed greatly to the company's success.

Quotation—Jack Schuessler, chief executive of Wendy's, based in the Columbus, Ohio suburb of Dublin: "He was the heart and soul of our company. He had a passion for great-tasting hamburgers and devoted his life to serving customers great food and helping those less fortunate in his community."

Quotation from Thomas—In 1991, he was quoted as saying: "As long as it works, I'll continue to do the commercials. When it's not working any longer, then I'm history."

More background—Thomas was born July 2, 1932. He was 12 when he got his first restaurant job. He worked as a counterman in Knoxville, Tenn. He was working at a barbecue restaurant in Fort Wayne, Ind., in 1956 when Col. Harland Sanders of Kentucky Fried Chicken fame stopped in on a promotional tour. At that time, Thomas' boss bought a KFC franchise. Six years later, Thomas moved to Columbus to take over four failing KFC restaurants. In 1968, he sold them back to the founder for $1.5 million when he was 35 years old.

About Wendy's—Thomas opened the first Wendy's Old Fashioned Hamburgers in Columbus in 1969. The restaurant was named for his 8-year-old daughter, Melinda Lou, who had been nicknamed Wendy by her siblings. The size of the chain at the time of his death: 6,000 restaurants worldwide. In 1996, Wendy's also acquired the Canadian-based Tim Hortons, a coffee and fresh-baked goods chain that has grown to more than 2,000 stores. Combined sales of both: $8 billion a year.

More quotations—Schuessler said: "Although Dave was wildly popular, he was never comfortable as a celebrity. He kept reminding us he was simply a hamburger cook."

More company background—During the middle 1980s, earnings dropped. Industry analysts and company officials credit his ads with helping the company rebound from the difficult period.

Quotation—Diane Mustain, a financial analyst, said in 1991, two years after the ads started running: "He's given Wendy's a corporate identity ... a down-homey type image. The lack of sophistication is a real benefit for the company."

His other interests—He created the Dave Thomas Foundation for Adoption, a not-for-profit organization. Thomas had been adopted as an infant. He became a national advocate for adoption. His organization was created to raise public awareness of adoption. He donated the profits from his books, *Dave's Way* and *Well Done!,* to the foundation.

Congressional testimony—Thomas once testified before Congress about the importance of creating incentives for adoption. He said during his testimony: "I know firsthand how important it is for every child to have a home and loving family. Without a family, I would not be where I am today."

6 Write an obit based on the following information, which is from an Associated Press story.

Name—Dick Schaap

Date of Death—Friday in New York

Age—67

Cause of death—From complications following hip surgery.

Background—He was a versatile electronic journalist, but was possibly best known for his sports work. His subjects covered a wide range—presidents, pitchers, governors and golfers. And others such as comedian Sid Caesar, who fought back from drug and alcohol addiction, and Bobby McLaughlin, a young man convicted of a murder he did not commit. He was well known for his Sunday morning ESPN show, *The Sports Reporters,* a lively debate with other journalists. The panelists seldom agreed. Schaap relished the energy that grew from the debates. His versatility was evident; he possibly was the only person who voted for the Heisman Trophy and the Tony Awards.

His awards—Included the Lifetime Achievement Award in Sports Journalism from the Crohn's and Colitis Foundation of America in 2001; the Northeastern Award for Excellence in Broadcast Sports Journalism in 1986; and the Women's Sports Foundation award for excellence in covering women's sports in 1984. He also found time to write more than 30 books.

Other awards—Three sports Emmy Awards for his work on ESPN and three Emmys for features on ABC's 20/20 and ABC's *World News Tonight,* where he worked for 20 years.

Quotation—ESPN President George Bodenheimer: "Dick's unparalleled journalistic achievements were exceeded only by his compassion and respect for his fellow human beings."

Survivors—His wife, Trish and five children, including his son, Jeremy, who works for ESPN.

7 Write an obit based on the following information, which is from an Associated Press story.

Name—King Hussein

Date of death—Sunday at 11:43 a.m.

Age—63

Cause of death—Lymphatic cancer. Fought a seven-month battle against the cancer. He had been unconscious on a respirator for two days after returning home to Jordan last week to die.

Services—Funeral to be held Monday, just 24 hours after his death, in keeping with Islamic tradition. The funeral will be an enormous procession through Amman.

Background—Jordan plunged into mourning for its beloved king. The weather was unusual as a rare, dripping fog shrouded the city after the king died. Distraught citizens sobbed in the streets. World leaders converged on the desert kingdom in an amazing united showing of grief for the statesman who built bridges for peace in the turbulent Middle East. Jordan crowned an untested new monarch: King Abdullah, Hussein's eldest son. King Abdullah is 37 years old. He was sworn in just four hours after the death of his father. He was sworn in before Parliament. Jordan was determined that the transition be swift and smooth.

Quotation—An announcer on Jordanian television said: "Even the sky is crying."

Description—Black flags fluttered from the few taxicabs on the streets. The wail of Koranic verses of mourning filled the country's mosques and residents wept openly on the sidewalks of Jordan's hilly capital.

Background—King Hussein was known for his far-reaching abilities as a mediator and leader—skills that lifted Jordan into a place of international prominence. Clearly, the respect for King Hussein was apparent because his elaborate state funeral drew people from around the world and across the political spectrum.

More background—Courtiers, Jordanian officials and members of the royal family had kept a vigil at the king's bedside for two days as thousands of citizens sobbed at the hospital gates. With him were his dozen children and his wife, the American-born Queen Noor.

More background—King Hussein had survived repeated assassination attempts as he walked the tightrope of Mideast politics. The tensions of the region were a factor in the elaborately plotted protocols of the state funeral. The Israeli delegation, for example, was scheduled to be kept closer to Western leaders than to leaders from harder-line Arab states, according to palace sources.

Quotation—King Abdullah, a veteran military man but a political novice, paused in front of the life-size portrait of his father and said: "This is God's judgment and God's will. God have mercy on Hussein the father, the brother, the commander and the man.... We will preserve Hussein's legacy."

More background—President Clinton and first lady Hillary Rodham Clinton were to be in attendance at the state funeral.

8 Write an obit based on the following information, which is from an Associated Press story.

Name—Gilda Radner

Date of death—Saturday at Cedars-Sinai Medical Center in Los Angeles

Age—42

Occupation—Entertainer

Cause of death—Cancer

Date of services—Private

Background—Miss Radner was a comedienne who was one of the original stars of "Saturday Night Live." She died in her sleep at about 6:20 a.m., according to hospital spokesman Ron Wise. She was the creator of such memorable characters as Roseanne Roseannadanna and Emily Litella. She was married to actor Gene Wilder, who was at her side when she died.

More background—She had recently completed a book about her battle against cancer. She told *Life* magazine in a 1988 interview: "Cancer is about the most unfunny thing in the world." She was a regular on "Saturday Night Live" from 1975 to 1980. She appeared on that program with such stars as Dan Aykroyd, Chevy Chase, Jane Curtin, Laraine Newman, Garrett Morris, Bill Murray and the late John Belushi.

More background—She had been diagnosed with ovarian cancer in 1986; she underwent nine months of chemotherapy. By 1988 the disease was in remission. She had undergone radiation therapy and other treatments as recently as February. She had also undergone surgery. According to Wise, she re-entered the hospital Wednesday. In recent years, she had appeared in several movies, but her fame was carved in NBC's "Saturday Night Live."

More background—Executive producer of "Saturday Night Live" is Lorne Michaels, who said that word of Miss Radner's death "stunned" everyone on the set. In fact, on Saturday night's show, host Steve Martin led off with a clip of a 1978 comedy routine that starred Miss Radner and him cavorting to "Dancing in the Dark" in a silent burlesque of Fred Astaire and Ginger Rogers.

Quotation—Martin's voice was thick with emotion when he told the "Saturday Night Live" audience: "When I look at that tape, I can't help but think how great she was, and how young I looked. Gilda, we miss you."

More background—According to family spokeswoman Rachel McCallister, memorial services will be private.

9 Write an obit based on the following information, which is from an Associated Press story.

Name—Richard Milhous Nixon

Date of death—Friday at 9:08 p.m. at New York Hospital

Age—81

Cause of death—Stroke that left him in a deep coma

Services—Scheduled for 4 p.m. Wednesday at the Richard M. Nixon Presidential Library and Birthplace in Yorba Linda, Calif. The Rev. Billy Graham, a family friend, to officiate. Private interment to follow at the library near his wife Pat Nixon's grave. Eulogies to be delivered by President Clinton, Sen. Bob Dole, R– Kan., and California Gov. Pete Wilson.

Details of death—Nixon died four days after suffering a stroke that had left him in a deep coma. His stroke apparently was the result of a blood clot that formed in his heart and moved to his brain's middle cerebral artery. The blockage deprived this crucial cranial region of oxygen, damaging some brain tissue and causing the swelling.

More details—His death was announced by Myrna Manners, a spokesperson for New York Hospital. She was quoted: "His family was with him." The announcement of his death came about 1½ hours after he died. The announcement was in the form of a two-sentence news release. After the announcement, the flag was lowered to half-staff over the White House. Reporters gathered outside the Manhattan hospital after his death was announced. By the time reporters arrived the body had been removed from the hospital. It was taken to an area funeral home. The body will not lie in state in the Capitol rotunda. The family wanted it that way. Family spokeswoman Liz Johnston said that Nixon had been involved in planning his funeral arrangements before his death. According to a statement issued from the Richard M. Nixon Presidential Library and Birthplace, the former president's body was to be flown to California on Tuesday to lie in state in the library's lobby. The public viewing will begin at 3 p.m. and then will continue through 11 a.m. Wednesday.

Quotation—Connecticut Gov. Lowell Weicker Jr., once a fierce critic of the Watergate scandal, said: "Past differences are now history. I wish him God's care and peace."

Quotation—President Clinton, who called a news conference in the Rose Garden to make the formal announcement, said: "I was deeply grateful to President Nixon for his wise counsel on many occasions. Our relationship continued to be warm and constructive.... He went out of his way to give me his best advice."

Quotation—From former President Ronald Reagan: "To Nancy and I he was a cherished friend and brilliant counselor. Richard Nixon understood the world. He understood politics, power and the fragile, yet undeniable force of history. There is no question that the legacy of this complicated and fascinating man will continue to guide the forces of democracy forever."

More background—Nixon suffered the stroke Monday night at his Park Ridge, N.J., home. He was partly paralyzed on the right side. He was unable to speak even before he slipped into the coma Thursday. His two daughters, Julie Eisenhower and Tricia Cox, both were at his side as his condition deteriorated. His wife, Pat, had died a year earlier. The Rev. Billy Graham also presided over that funeral. All three networks interrupted regular programming to announce the death. They also presented highlights of his career.

Survivors—Daughters Tricia and Julie, sons-in-law Edward F. Cox and David Eisenhower, and grandchildren Christopher Cox and Jennie Elizabeth, Alex Richard and Melanie Eisenhower.

10 Write an obit based on the following information, which is from an Associated Press story.

Name—James Reston

Date of death—Wednesday at his home in Washington, D.C.

Age—86

Cause of death—Cancer after a long illness, according to his son, Thomas Reston

Services—Pending

Background—Reston was a two-time Pulitzer Prize winner for *The New York Times.* He was a columnist and Washington bureau chief who covered national and international affairs for about 50 years. He helped create the nation's first Op-Ed page. That was in 1970. The Op-Ed page is the page across from newspaper editorials. It forms a stage for columnists' opinion pieces. He was chief of the *Times'* Washington bureau from 1953 to 1974. He then spent his time writing columns after serving briefly as the newspaper's executive editor in New York. He wrote his last column for the *Times* in 1987. He retired in 1989.

His Pulitzer Prizes—The first came when he obtained the Allies' secret proposals at the 1944 Dumbarton Oaks conference on planning the United Nations. He won his second for covering the 1956 presidential campaign.

More background—He was born in Clydebank, Scotland. He came to the United States with his parents when he was 11 years old. His newspaper career was launched as a reporter on the *Springfield* (Ohio) *Daily News* in 1932. He later was a sports writer for The Associated Press in New York and London. He went to work for *The New York Times* in 1938. He transferred to Washington in 1941. He succeeded Arthur Krock as Washington bureau chief. Reston hired several people who went on to become big names in journalism: Tom Wicker, Anthony Lewis, Allen Drury and Russell Baker.

Quotation—From R. W. Apple, Washington bureau chief for the *Times:* "He was the greatest journalist of his generation. And he recruited and trained two more generations of journalists at the *Times* and elsewhere."

Quotation—From *Washington Post* Publisher Donald Graham: "Scotty Reston was a great columnist and a great man. He broke many of the biggest stories of his time, and hired many of the best reporters. I never knew anyone more deeply admired by those who knew him best."

11 Write an obit based on the following information, which is from an Associated Press story.

Name—Lewis F. Powell

Date of death—Tuesday at his home in Richmond, Va.

Age—90

Cause of death—Pneumonia. Died in his sleep at 4:30 a.m., the Supreme Court said in a statement.

Background—Powell was a retired Supreme Court justice. He was known as someone who did not actively seek an appointment to the Supreme Court. But President Richard Nixon appointed him and Powell agreed to serve. He left a big footprint because he was the deciding voice in several 5–4 votes in which he was pivotal for the majority.

Best-known cases in which he was pivotal for the majority in 5–4 votes—That consenting adults do not enjoy a constitutional right to private homosexual conduct. (Powell said after his retirement that he "probably made a mistake" with his vote in the 1986 Georgia sodomy case.) That medical school applicant Allan Bakke suffered unlawful discrimination because he was white. That presidents enjoy "absolute immunity" from being sued for monetary damages if their misconduct in office was within their official duties. (That decision was handed down during the Nixon administration.)

More background—He retired from the court in 1987 but maintained his office for 10 more years. Because his health was poor recently, he closed his Supreme Court office about 18 months prior to his death.

Quotation—President Clinton said: Powell "approached each case without an ideological agenda, carefully applying the Constitution, the law and Supreme Court precedent regardless of his own personal views. His opinions were a model of balance and judiciousness."

Quotation—John C. Jeffries, his biographer and former law clerk, said: "He was a traditional lawyer ... he reasoned from the bottom up. He developed a habit of listening and tried to make up his mind slowly."

His appearance—Justice Powell was slight and bespectacled.

His legacy opinion—The Bakke case, a decision that upheld the concept of affirmative action while limiting its scope—a delicate but so-far durable balance.

More background—When President Nixon nominated him to the court, Powell had a reputation as a conservative. When he joined the court in 1972, it was ideologically divided. He served for 15 years on the court. Because the court was ideologically divided during much of that time, his non-ideological agenda on several occasions made him the key vote in close decisions. He never closely aligned with exclusively conservative or liberal views during his years on the court.

14

News Releases

Review Questions

1 Each day, journalists have to go through a stack of news releases to decide which are worth printing or broadcasting and which are not. What are four factors that determine whether a news release will be used or tossed into the wastebasket?

a

b

c

d

2 What are the five things *ereleases.com* urges writers do to improve the chances of their press releases being used?

3 Discuss the phrase "eliminate the fluff."

4 Why is "local news value" important when determining the newsworthiness of a news release?

Suggested Exercises

1 Write a two-paragraph news story from the information provided in the following news release.

MONTHLY MEETING
Organization: Phoenix Chapter of the Arizona Archaeological Society

Date of meeting: Thursday, May 8

Time: 7:30 to 9:00 P.M.

Place: Pueblo Grande Museum, 4619 E. Washington, Phoenix

Speaker: Dr. Ron Gould, Project Director of Soil Systems Inc.

Topic of Program: Dr. Gould will present a slide lecture on Squaw Peak Parkway archaeology. He will present an overview of the work that has been done, including information on the ceramics.

Remarks: Dr. Gould is a ceramicist, having received his B.A. and M.A. from Wichita State University and his Ph.D. from the University of Texas. He has worked in Kansas, Texas and Colorado.

THE LECTURE IS FREE
AND THE PUBLIC IS INVITED.

James M. Brown, Public Relations Chairman

Phone: 279-9226

2 Rewrite the following news release into a three-paragraph news story.

GENERAL RELEASE

Contact: Scott A. Miller (570-662-4844)

For immediate release

MANSFIELD, PA—Mansfield University will celebrate Black History Month with an African-American Arts Festival, Feb. 14 to March 15, featuring music, art, films, a unique workshop, performances and poetry readings.

Events begin with a bus trip for MU students Sunday, Feb. 14, to Elmira's Clemens Center for a 7 p.m. "Blast from the Past" concert featuring three seminal vocal groups: The Drifters, The Platters, and The Coasters.

On Monday, Feb. 15, at 10:30 a.m. in Manser Hall's North Dining Room, SST Communications of Chicago will present the fun, hard-hitting and dramatic workshop "What's So Different About Diversity?" The live theatre presentation teaches diversity with humor and drama performed by professional actors.

The workshop's goal is to "change the way you think about othrs." It's free and open to all faculty, staff and students, and is sponsored by the human resources and affirmative action offices, as well as the President's Advisory Board for Diversity.

On Tuesday, Feb. 16, from 11 a.m.–1 p.m. in The Hut, student Richard Newton-Morris and friends will give a poetry reading.

On Wednesday, Feb. 17, at 8 p.m. in Allen Lecture Hall, the festival will present "Just Another Girl on the I.R.T.," a critically acclaimed film directed by Leslie Harris. Andrew Longoria, communication and theatre, will give a talk on the "History of African-American Actors and Directors in Film and Theater" prior to the film, which is free and open to the public.

On Thursday, Feb. 18, at 7 p.m., in Allen Lecture Hall, the festival will team with the MU Film Series to present the Jonathan Demme film "Beloved," based on the award-winning novel by Toni Morrison. The film series is sponsored by the Provost's Office and the Mansfield Activities Council.

An African-American Artists Exhibit opens Saturday, Feb. 20, from 9 a.m.–4 p.m. at First Citizens National Bank, Main Street, Mansfield, and continues through Feb. 27.

On Sunday, Feb. 21, an exhibit of work by artist Reginald Fatherly will open with a reception from 2–4 p.m. in the University Gallery of North Hall.

The Nommo Performing Arts Company, a group of Penn State students, will bring its unique combination of dance, theater and music to campus for a show Monday, Feb. 22, at 7 p.m. in Steadman Theatre. The company formed in 1965 in part motivated by the lack of Black representation in Penn State's theater arts department programs. It has since grown to more than 30 members and regularly performs traditional and original works that reflect the culture and traditions of Africans and African-Americans.

Manser Lobby will host an exhibit and sale of African art from 10 a.m.–2 p.m., Feb. 23–25.

On Tuesday, Feb. 23, at 7 p.m. in Allen Hall 111, J. McGee and H. R. Carter will speak on the "History of African-American Artists."

The final event in the festival is a musical performance titled "Beehive," a professional tour by Encore Attractions featuring the music of the 1960s. The show is Monday, March 15, at 8 p.m. in Straughn Hall. It is free for all MU students; $7.50 for all others. For ticket information call 570-662-4980.

All events are free and open to the public unless otherwise noted. The African-American Arts Festival is sponsored by Mansfield Activities Council, Student Activities Office, Mansfield University, and by a social equity grant from the State System of Higher Education Office of the Chancellor.

3 Boil down the following news release, and write a brief news story.

DU PONT NEWS

Du Pont Company/External Affairs Department/ Wilmington, Delaware 19898

FOR IMMEDIATE RELEASE

CONTACTS:

Alan Trei
Du Pont
(302) 999-2792
or
Holly Chung
Burson-Marsteller
(212) 614-4305

DU PONT ACCEPTING ENTRIES FOR "ANTRON" DESIGN AWARDS

Entries are now being accepted for the annual Du Pont "Antron" Student Design Award competition. Students at U.S. accredited schools of interior design and architecture nationwide are eligible.

The competition offers students a chance to gain important recognition from the professional design community, as well as a grand prize of $1,000 and category awards of $500 each, all with matching funds to winners' schools.

The winners will be honored among some of America's leading professional designers at special ceremonies in New York City before several dozen top editors of design publications and in Chicago at NEOCON 22, one of the most important trade shows in the commercial interior design industry. Winners' travel expenses are paid by Du Pont.

Participants are required to design a commercial environment, providing the judges with a rendering and a written rationale. The design must incorporate carpet of 100 percent Du Pont "Antron," "Antron" XL or "Antron Precedent" nylon as an important design element; carpet and fabric samples must also be submitted.

Entries will be judged in the categories of offices, hospitality facilities, health-care facilities, public spaces and store planning spaces. Entry deadline is February 15.

Last year's grand prize winner, Kathleen Johnstone of Syracuse University was "wined and dined" in New York and at NEOCON in Chicago, where she shared the stage with the rock duo Daryl Hall & John Oates during a Du Pont-sponsored show honoring the student and professional design award winners.

Johnstone's picture and stories featuring her winning entry also appeared in *Interior Design* and various floorcovering trade magazines.

"Winning the grand-prize in the Du Point 'Antron' Design Award helped me meet leaders in the design community," Johnstone said, "which is something that every recent college graduate needs when looking for their first job opportunity.

"As a result of winning this award, I showed my portfolio to Stanford Hughes, one of the judges and was hired by his firm, the San Francisco office of Skidmore, Owings & Merrill. The 'Antron' award really changed my life."

For entry forms and more information on this year's competition, please see your design professor, ASID student chapter president, or contact Holly Chung at the Du Pont "Antron" Student Design Award Center, (212) 614-4305.

4 Boil down the following news release, and write a brief news story.

JOHNS HOPKINS UNIVERSITY NEWS
News and Information Services
Baltimore, Maryland 21218

FOR IMMEDIATE RELEASE

CONTACT: Lisa Hooker
(301) 338-7160

DONORS' FIRST BLOOD IS OFTEN THEIR LAST, SAYS HOPKINS PSYCHOLOGIST

"Almost half of the people in this country have donated blood at least once," said Steven Breckler, associate professor of psychology at The Johns Hopkins University, "but the vast majority of those people have donated only once, and most of them will never donate again."

Breckler, named a Presidential Young Investigator earlier this year by the National Science Foundation, currently is working to determine why this is so, and to find ways of converting one-time blood donors to the ranks of veteran donors. Supported by a grant from the American Red Cross, Breckler and graduate student Beth Wiggins plan to follow Maryland bloodmobiles to a number of blood-collection centers, including drives at churches, industrial centers, and military headquarters. They already have visited blood drives at Hopkins' own Glass Pavilion, where they began their research two and a half years ago.

A major factor in one-time donors' unwillingness to give again, Breckler believes, is that they are likely to remember only the bad things about their first experience. The temporary high, the "warm glow," one gets from donating blood is short-lived: "A couple of days or weeks later, what you tend to remember are the most salient aspects of having donated blood, the dizziness and the inconvenience."

Breckler also noted that the Red Cross tries to downplay the possibility of a donor's feeling dizzy or weak after giving blood, whereas in fact many people experience these reactions. A frank explanation of how he can expect to feel, he said, could make a neophyte donor more comfortable with his experience, and thus encourage him to return.

A Harris poll of more than 1,200 people concluded that 46 percent had donated blood once. However, the Red Cross is able to persuade only 14 percent of all first-time donors to return.

Although the advent of the AIDS crisis caused a temporary dip in the levels of blood being donated, Breckler said, it appears to have had little lasting effect on people's willingness to give.

Breckler and Wiggins originally took verbal reports from donors for their studies, but they now plan to employ more sophisticated methods for measuring responses, including the analysis of facial expression and tone of voice. The Facial Action Coding System, for example, provides a means for quantifying facial expressions by looking at the movement or setting of various muscles.

With FACS, every muscle in the face is coded, and reactions are determined by which muscles are used in an expression. "Facial expressions often give you away, and it's frequently possible to tell even if people are faking, because a fake smile often involves different muscles than a real smile."

Donors may often hide their true feelings about giving blood when asked, because they want to appear brave and generous, Breckler said. In reality, they may be feeling fear, disgust or pain.

The results of his studies of blood donors, Breckler believes, have significant implications for the field of attitude theory. He has found, for instance, that there is a much stronger relationship between donors' emotions and their behavior than between their thoughts and beliefs and their behavior.

"That's a very interesting result," he said, "because a lot of social psychology and psychology in general is guided by the assumption that behavior is rationally determined, that you think and you intend to do things, and then you do them. But we've found emotion weighs even more heavily than beliefs."

5 Boil down the following news release, and write a brief news story.

HERBERGER THEATER CENTER

FOR IMMEDIATE RELEASE

Further Information:
Leon E. Scioscla
602-254-7399

HERBERGER THEATER CENTER AND CENTER DANCE ENSEMBLE ANNOUNCE A MODERN DANCE WORKSHOP WITH MASTER TEACHER—ETHEL BUTLER

Master Teacher, Ethel Butler, will be holding a modern dance workshop in conjunction with Center Dance Ensemble. Frances Smith Cohen, Artistic Director of Center Dance Ensemble, is pleased to be hosting this workshop with this legendary dancer/teacher.

Ms. Butler began her dance career with Martha Graham in New York City in 1932 and was the only acknowledged teacher for the Graham company for the first 8 years of its existence. From 1932 to 1944 Ms. Butler danced in such classics as Primitive Mysteries 1932, Celebration 1934 and Letter to the World 1940.

Her students included Yuriko, Paul Taylor, Ethel Winter and Merce Cunningham. In 1944 she relocated in Washington, D.C., where she became a leading force in modern dance for the next thirty years. She directed the Ethel Butler Dance Company, established the only professional dance studio in Washington and taught choreography and technique at Howard University.

Retiring her studio in 1972, Ms. Butler became a choreographer consultant and master teacher at the University of Maryland where she continues to teach advanced technique classes and teaches master workshops around the country.

Ms. Cohen said: "This is our way to open up our first full year of existence. We're excited and pleased to have a person of this caliber come in and work with our students."

The workshop runs from August 21–August 25 between the hours of 9:30 AM-11:00AM in the Herberger Theater Center Rehearsal Room. The fee for 5 classes is $40.00 or $10.00 for each individual class. The workshop is for intermediate and advanced dancers. For complete workshop information please call: Frances Smith Cohen at 996-9027.

6 Use the following information to write a news release for immediate release.

What: Maricopa County, the largest county in Arizona, which takes in the metropolitan Phoenix area, is holding a special bond election on May 6.

Hours: Polls open at 6 a.m. and close at 7 p.m.

Locations of Elections Central: The Supervisors Auditorium at the Maricopa County Complex, 205 W. Jefferson, Phoenix. Doors will open for media access at 6 p.m. on election day.

Elections Central: Central reporting station for updated election results with telephones, hook-ups, and private area available to the media. Elections Central will be open to the public. Any citizen interested in knowing election results and viewing the election process is invited.

First results: First election results will be available at 8:30 p.m. Election results will be displayed on a tally screen as they are received and will be updated by the Elections Department staff every 15 minutes beginning at 8:30 p.m.

Number of eligible voters: 825,746.

Number of polling places: 1,093.

Number of official receiving stations: Eleven. Increased from four in the last general election for the metro Phoenix area, in a continuing effort by the Elections Department to expedite the dissemination of election results.

Vote count procedure: Punch card voting system with tabulation at Maricopa County Complex, Department of Computer Services.

Official prediction of voter turnout: County Recorder Keith Poletis is forecasting that 9.7%, or 80,097, of the county's registered voters will cast ballots. This represents 6% of the county's voting age population.

Quotations from Poletis: "There is every indication that we are due for a disappointing voter turnout on May 6. I hope that I am wrong. I hope that my prediction doesn't come true, but the numbers are pointing to a low turnout in this election.

"The projected low voter turnout indicates, at a minimum, that election law reform is essential to facilitate and encourage voting. All governments must do more to ensure greater voter participation."

Maricopa County recorder: The Maricopa County recorder is the official registrar of voters and supervises the county's Elections Department, which is responsible for all federal, state and county elections in Maricopa County.

Summary of campaign issue: Voters are being asked to approve the sale of $261 million in Maricopa County general obligation bonds to provide revenue for capital improvements.

Finance: This election is being paid for by Maricopa County at a cost of $899,000.

Last countywide election: Special Transportation issue held in October. That election saw a record high turnout for a special election with 34% of the registered voters casting ballots.

Further information or sample ballot: Available by calling the Elections Department at 262-1511 from 8 a.m. to 5 p.m. Mondays through Fridays.

Media contacts:

Keith Poletis
Maricopa County Recorder
262-3628

Barbara Lebsch
Special Assistant to County Recorder
262-3634

Jer Inderieden
Public Information Office
262-3272

15

Speeches and Press Conferences

Review Questions

1 What are the advantages and disadvantages of using an advance text of a speech?

2 Discuss the steps that a reporter should follow when covering a speech.

3 What questions must a reporter answer before writing a speech story?

4 Why do candidates, officials and other people hold press conferences?

5 What is a *gang interview?*

6 Discuss the development of the presidential press conference.

7 Discuss the procedures that reporters should follow in preparing for a press conference.

8 What is an advance?

9 Television reporters have an advantage over print reporters during a press conference because the speaker usually wants to be seen as well as heard. What can print reporters do to make themselves visible and heard?

10 How is covering a speech different from covering a press conference?

1 Following is a large portion of President George W. Bush's 2002 State of the Union Address to Congress. Read the speech, and then write a news story as though you covered the speech in person today and are writing for tomorrow morning's paper.

As we gather tonight, our nation is at war, our economy is in recession and the civilized world faces unprecedented dangers. Yet the state of our union has never been stronger.

We last met in an hour of shock and suffering. In four short months, our nation has comforted the victims, begun to rebuild New York and the Pentagon, rallied a great coalition, captured, arrested and rid the world of thousands of terrorists, destroyed Afghanistan's terrorist training camps, saved a people from starvation and freed a country from brutal oppression.

The American flag flies again over our embassy in Kabul. Terrorists who once occupied Afghanistan now occupy cells at Guantanamo Bay. And terrorist leaders who urged followers to sacrifice their lives are running for their own.

America and Afghanistan are now allies against terror. We'll be partners in rebuilding that country, and this evening we welcomed the distinguished interim leader of a liberated Afghanistan, Chairman Hamid Karzai.

The last time we met in this chamber, the mothers and daughters of Afghanistan were captives in their own homes, forbidden from working or going to school. Today women are free, and are part of Afghanistan's new government, and we welcome the new minister of women's affairs, Dr. Sima Samar.

Our progress is a tribute to the spirit of the Afghan people, to the resolve of our coalition and to the might of the United States military.

When I called our troops into action, I did so with complete confidence in their courage and skill, and tonight, thanks to them, we are winning the war on terror. The men and women of our armed forces have delivered a message now clear to every enemy of the United States: Even 7,000 miles away, across oceans and continents, on mountaintops and in caves, you will not escape the justice of this nation.

For many Americans, these four months have brought sorrow and pain that will never completely go away. Every day a retired firefighter returns to Ground Zero, to feel closer to his two sons who died there. At a memorial in New York, a little boy left his football with a note for his lost father: "Dear Daddy, please take this to Heaven. I don't want to play football until I can play with you again someday." Last month, at the grave of her husband, Micheal, CIA officer and Marine who died in Mazar-i-Sharif, Shannon Spann said these words of farewell: "Semper Fi, my love." Shannon is with us tonight.

Shannon, I assure you and all who have lost a loved one that our cause is just and our country will never forget the debt we owe Micheal and all who gave their lives for freedom.

Our cause is just, and it continues. Our discoveries in Afghanistan confirmed our worst fears and showed us the true scope of the task ahead. We have seen the depth of our enemies' hatred in videos where they laugh about the loss of innocent life. And the depth of their hatred is equaled by the madness of the destruction they design. We have found diagrams of American nuclear power plants and public water facilities, detailed instructions for making chemical weapons, surveillance maps of American cities and thorough descriptions of landmarks in America and throughout the world.

What we have found in Afghanistan confirms that, far from ending there, our war against terror is only beginning. Most of the 19 men who hijacked planes on Sept. 11 were trained in Afghanistan's camps, and so were tens of thousands of others. Thousands of dangerous killers, schooled in the methods of murder, often supported by outlaw regimes, are now spread throughout the world like ticking time bombs, set to go off without warning.

Thanks to the work of our law enforcement officials and coalition partners, hundreds of terrorists have been arrested, yet tens of thousands of trained terrorists are still at large. These enemies view the entire world as a battlefield, and we must pursue them wherever they are. So long as training camps operate, so long as nations harbor terrorists, freedom is at risk, and America and our allies must not, and will not, allow it.

Our nation will continue to be steadfast and patient and persistent in the pursuit of two great objectives. First, we will shut down terrorist camps, disrupt terrorist plans and bring terrorists to justice. And second, we must prevent the terrorists and regimes who seek chemical, biological, or nuclear weapons from threatening the United States and the world.

Our military has put the terror training camps of Afghanistan out of business, yet camps still exist in at least a dozen countries. A terrorist underworld, including groups like Hamas, Hezbollah, Islamic Jihad, Jaish-e-Muhammad, operates in remote jungles and deserts, and hides in the centers of large cities.

While the most visible military action is in Afghanistan, America is acting elsewhere. We now have troops in the Philippines helping to train that country's armed forces to go after terrorist cells that have executed an American and still hold hostages. Our soldiers, working with the Bosnian government, seized terrorists who were plotting to bomb our embassy. Our Navy is patrolling the coast of Africa to block the shipment of weapons and the establishment of terrorist camps in Somalia.

My hope is that all nations will heed our call, and eliminate the terrorist parasites who threaten their countries, and our own. Many nations are acting forcefully. Pakistan is now cracking down on terror, and I admire the strong leadership of President Musharraf. But some governments will be timid in the face of terror. And make no mistake about it: If they do not act, America will.

Our second goal is to prevent regimes that sponsor terror from threatening America or our friends and allies with weapons of mass destruction.

Some of these regimes have been pretty quiet since Sept. 11. But we know their true nature. North Korea is a regime arming with missiles and weapons of mass destruction, while starving its citizens.

Iran aggressively pursues these weapons and exports terror, while an unelected few repress the Iranian people's hope for freedom.

Iraq continues to flaunt its hostility toward America and to support terror. The Iraqi regime has plotted to develop anthrax and nerve gas and nuclear weapons for over a decade. This is a regime that has already used poison gas to murder thousands of its own citizens, leaving the bodies of mothers huddled over their dead children. This is a regime that agreed to international inspections, then kicked out the inspectors. This is a regime that has something to hide from the civilized world.

States like these, and their terrorist allies, constitute an axis of evil, arming to threaten the peace of the world. By seeking weapons of mass destruction, these regimes pose a grave and growing danger. They could provide these arms to terrorists, giving them the means to match their hatred. They could attack our allies or attempt to blackmail the United States. In any of these cases, the price of indifference would be catastrophic.

We will work closely with our coalition to deny terrorists and their state sponsors the materials, technology, and expertise to make and deliver weapons of mass destruction. We will develop and deploy effective missile defenses to protect America and our allies from sudden attack. And all nations should know: America will do what is necessary to ensure our nation's security.

History has called America and our allies to action, and it is both our responsibility and our privilege to fight freedom's fight.

Our first priority must always be the security of our nation, and that will be reflected in the budget I send to Congress. My budget supports three great goals for

America: We will win this war, we'll protect our homeland and we will revive our economy.

Sept. 11 brought out the best in America, and the best in this Congress, and I join the American people in applauding your unity and resolve.

Now Americans deserve to have this same spirit directed toward addressing problems here at home. I'm a proud member of my party. Yet as we act to win the war, protect our people and create jobs in America, we must act first and foremost not as Republicans, not as Democrats, but as Americans.

It costs a lot to fight this war. We have spent more than a billion dollars a month, over $30 million a day, and we must be prepared for future operations. Afghanistan proved that expensive precision weapons defeat the enemy and spare innocent lives, and we need more of them. We need to replace aging aircraft and make our military more agile to put our troops anywhere in the world quickly and safely. Our men and women in uniform deserve the best weapons, the best equipment, the best training, and they also deserve another pay raise. My budget includes the largest increase in defense spending in two decades, because while the price of freedom and security is high, it is never too high. Whatever it costs to defend our country, we will pay.

The next priority of my budget is to do everything possible to protect our citizens and strengthen our nation against the ongoing threat of another attack.

Time and distance from the events of Sept. 11 will not make us safer unless we act on its lessons. America is no longer protected by vast oceans. We are protected from attack only by vigorous action abroad, and increased vigilance at home.

My budget nearly doubles funding for a sustained strategy of homeland security, focused on four key areas: bioterrorism, emergency response, airport and border security, and improved intelligence. We will develop vaccines to fight anthrax and other deadly diseases. We'll increase funding to help states and communities train and equip our heroic police and firefighters. We will improve intelligence collection and sharing, expand patrols at our borders, strengthen the security of air travel and use technology to track the arrivals and departures of visitors to the United States.

Homeland security will make America not only stronger, but in many ways better. Knowledge gained from bioterrorism research will improve public health; stronger police and fire departments will mean safer neighborhoods; stricter border enforcement will help combat illegal drugs.

Once we have funded our national security and our homeland security, the final great priority of my budget is economic security for the American people.

To achieve these great national objectives—to win the war, protect the homeland and revitalize our economy—our budget will run a deficit that will be small and short term so long as Congress restrains spending and acts in a fiscally responsible manner. We have clear priorities, and we must act at home with the same purpose and resolve we have shown overseas. We will prevail in the war and we will defeat this recession.

Americans who've lost their jobs need our help. And I support extending unemployment benefits and direct assistance for health care coverage. Yet American workers want more than unemployment checks, they want a steady paycheck. When America works, America prospers, so my economic security plan can be summed up in one word: jobs.

Good jobs begin with good schools, and here we've made a fine start.

Republicans and Democrats worked together to achieve historic education reform so that no child is left behind. I was proud to work with members of both parties, Chairman John Boehner and Congressman George Miller, Senator Judd Gregg. And I was so proud of our work I even had nice things to say about my friend Ted Kennedy. I know the folks at the Crawford coffee shop couldn't believe I'd say such a thing. But our work on this bill shows what is possible if we set aside posturing and focus on results.

There is more to do. We need to prepare

our children to read and succeed in school with improved Head Start and early childhood development programs. We must upgrade our teacher colleges and teacher training and launch a major recruiting drive with a great goal for America, a quality teacher in every classroom.

Good jobs also depend on reliable and affordable energy. This Congress must act to encourage conservation, promote technology, build infrastructure, and it must act to increase energy production at home so America is less dependent on foreign oil.

Good jobs depend on expanded trade. Selling into new markets creates new jobs, so I ask Congress to finally approve trade promotion authority. On these two key issues, trade and energy, the House of Representatives has acted to create jobs, and I urge the Senate to pass this legislation.

Good jobs depend on sound tax policy. Last year, some in this hall thought my tax relief plan was too small; some thought it was too big. But when the checks arrived in the mail, most Americans thought tax relief was just about right. Congress listened to the people and responded by reducing tax rates, doubling the child credit and ending the death tax. For the sake of long-term growth and to help Americans plan for the future, let's make these tax cuts permanent.

The way out of this recession, the way to create jobs, is to grow the economy by encouraging investment in factories and equipment, and by speeding up tax relief so people have more money to spend. For the sake of American workers, let's pass a stimulus package.

Good jobs must be the aim of welfare reform. As we reauthorize these important reforms, we must always remember the goal is to reduce dependency on government and offer every American the dignity of a job.

Americans know economic security can vanish in an instant without health security. I ask Congress to join me this year to enact a patients' bill of rights, to give uninsured workers credits to help buy health coverage, to approve an historic increase in the spending for veterans' health, and to give seniors a sound and modem Medicare system that includes coverage for prescription drugs.

Members, you and I will work together in the months ahead on other issues: productive farm policy, a cleaner environment, broader home ownership, especially among minorities, and ways to encourage the good work of charities and faith-based groups. I ask you to join me on these important domestic issues in the same spirit of cooperation we have applied to our war against terrorism.

During these last few months, I have been humbled and privileged to see the true character of this country in a time of testing. Our enemies believed America was weak and materialistic, that we would splinter in fear and selfishness. They were as wrong as they are evil.

The American people have responded magnificently, with courage and compassion, strength and resolve. As I have met the heroes, hugged the families, and looked into the tired faces of rescuers, I have stood in awe of the American people.

And I hope you will join me in expressing thanks to one American for the strength, and calm, and comfort she brings to our nation in crisis: our first lady, Laura Bush.

None of us would ever wish the evil that was done on Sept. 11, yet after America was attacked, it was as if our entire country looked into a mirror, and saw our better selves. We were reminded that we are citizens, with obligations to each other, to our country, and to history. We began to think less of the goods we can accumulate, and more about the good we can do. For too long our culture has said, "If it feels good, do it." Now America is embracing a new ethic and a new creed: "Let's roll." In the sacrifice of soldiers, the fierce brotherhood of firefighters and the bravery and generosity of ordinary citizens, we have glimpsed what a new culture of responsibility could look like. We want to be a nation that serves goals larger than self. We've been offered a unique opportunity, and we must not let this moment pass.

My call tonight is for every American to commit at least two years, four thousand hours over the rest of your lifetime, to the service of your neighbors and your nation.

Many are already serving and I thank you. If you aren't sure how to help, I've got a good place to start. To sustain and extend the best that has emerged in America, I invite you to join the new U.S.A. Freedom Corps. The Freedom Corps will focus on three areas of need: responding in case of crisis at home, rebuilding our communities and extending American compassion throughout the world.

One purpose of the U.S.A. Freedom Corps will be homeland security. America needs retired doctors and nurses who can be mobilized in major emergencies, volunteers to help police and fire departments, transportation and utility workers well-trained in spotting danger.

Our country also needs citizens working to rebuild our communities. We need mentors to love children, especially children whose parents are in prison, and we need more talented teachers in troubled schools. U.S.A. Freedom Corps will expand and improve the good efforts of AmeriCorps and Senior Corps to recruit more than 200,000 new volunteers.

And America needs citizens to extend the compassion of our country to every part of the world. So we will renew the promise of the Peace Corps, double its volunteers over the next five years and ask it to join a new effort to encourage development and education and opportunity in the Islamic world.

America will take the side of brave men and women who advocate these values around the world, including the Islamic world, because we have a greater objective than eliminating threats and containing resentment. We seek a just and peaceful world beyond the war on terror.

In this moment of opportunity, a common danger is erasing old rivalries.

America is working with Russia and China and India in ways we never have before to achieve peace and prosperity. In every region, free markets and free trade and free societies are proving their power to lift lives. Together with friends and allies, from Europe to Asia and Africa to Latin America, we will demonstrate that the forces of terror cannot stop the momentum of freedom.

The last time I spoke here, I expressed the hope that life would return to normal. In some ways, it has. In others, it never will. Those of us who have lived through these challenging times have been changed by them. We've come to know truths that we will never question: Evil is real, and it must be opposed.

Beyond all differences of race or creed, we are one country, mourning together and facing danger together. Deep in the American character, there is honor, and it is stronger than cynicism. And many have discovered again that even in tragedy, especially in tragedy, God is near.

In a single instant, we realized that this will be a decisive decade in the history of liberty, that we've been called to a unique role in human events.

Rarely has the world faced a choice more clear or consequential.

Our enemies send other people's children on missions of suicide and murder.

They embrace tyranny and death as a cause and a creed. We stand for a different choice, made long ago, on the day of our founding. We affirm it again today. We choose freedom and the dignity of every life.

Steadfast in our purpose, we now press on. We have known freedom's price.

We have shown freedom's power. And in this great conflict, my fellow Americans, we will see freedom's victory. Thank you all. May God bless.

2 Following is the transcript of a portion of a press conference between presidential spokesman Ari Fleischer and the White House press corps. The meeting was held in the James S. Brady Briefing Room early in 2002. Read the transcript as though you were a reporter in the room and that you now must write a story. You can presume that it was held today and that you are writing the story for a morning newspaper tomorrow. Also make sure you follow AP style when you write the story (note that president is lower case as a title standing alone). You also will have to look up the first names of people mentioned by Fleischer, should you decide to use them in your story.

MR. FLEISCHER: Good afternoon. Let me give you a report on the President's day, then I'll be happy to take your questions.

The President this morning spoke with President Mubarak of Egypt for about 15 minutes. They discussed the situation in the Middle East. President Bush made clear his disappointment with Chairman Arafat, including Chairman Arafat's failure to crack down on terrorism.

The two leaders emphasized the importance of peace and stability in the region. They both reaffirmed their commitment to continue to work towards this end, and they also agreed to continue close consultations between the United States and Egypt.

Following the call to President Mubarak, the President received a CIA and FBI briefing, then he convened a meeting of the National Security Council. The President will shortly be meeting with the Chairman of the Afghan Interim Authority, Hamid Karzai, in an Oval Office meeting. And then the President will proceed to the Rose Garden, where the two will make a statement to the press and take questions.

Following this, the President this afternoon will return to the domestic agenda, and the President will meet with various members of Congress to talk about strengthening and modernizing Medicare. And that's a report on the President's day; I'm happy to take your questions.

Q Ari, in the NSC meeting today, did this issue of treatment of the prisoners down in Guantanamo Bay come up? And can you describe a little bit how the President is wading through the disagreement among other officials about how to treat them and whether they are subject to the Geneva accords?

MR. FLEISCHER: Okay. Let me answer that to the best degree I can, David; I want to proceed with care. As you know, it is the longstanding policy that we don't talk about what's discussed in NSC meetings.

Having said that to be helpful, as you know, it's been publicly indicated by others, as for the people who are the detainees who are being held in Cuba, the determination has been made that they are not and will not be considered POWs. That in the tradition of this country, and it should go without saying, that anybody in the custody of our military will, at all times, be treated humanely. That is the American way.

As for some of the legal issues involving the applicability of the Geneva Convention, the President received the advice of his counsel and the President has made no determinations, having received that advice.

Q Can you explain what the advice was?

MR. FLEISCHER: No, I cannot get into any individual's advice to the President in an NSC meeting.

Q Can I follow on another point? In the context of disclosures regarding energy policy to the GAO, you have talked about the principle involved and how this would be viewed going forward. What about the concern about the principles involved in the treatment of detainees and how, rightly or wrongly, that may be seen by others around the world that could ultimately affect service personnel of the United States, or other Americans and their treatment?

MR. FLEISCHER: Aside from the fact that everything the government does should involve principles, I don't see the connection between the two. But the United States military, for hundreds of years, has always honored the traditions and the high calling of this nation to treat people well. And that's exactly what's happening in Cuba.

In Cuba, as a result of terrorists who moved to Afghanistan from other countries to be taught and trained in the art of how to kill innocents, how to blow themselves up and commit suicide in a way that takes the lives of others, these people were captured in terrorist camps and terrorist bases, at which they located themselves in Afghanistan. They fought in a war against the United States in which we had our men and women on the ground fighting. And for these people who are now detainees, the choice was either, be captured or be killed. And they've been captured.

And in being captured, they're lucky to be in the custody of our military, because they're receiving three square meals a day, they're receiving health care that they never received before. Their sleeping conditions are probably better than anything they've had in Afghanistan. And they're being treated well because they're in the hands of the men and women of our military. And they're being treated well, because that's what Americans do.

Within that there are legal issues that involve the Geneva Convention that are being looked at. And as I mentioned, they are going to always be treated humanely. They are not going to be considered POWs. They will be allowed, for example, to receive and to send correspondence. They will be allowed to receive and send—receive food and clothing, subject to proper security clearance screenings.

But one of the things, for example, if they were POWs, that they'd be entitled to, which they are not going to get, is going to be a stipend for tobacco. Those are things they would be entitled to. They'd be entitled to advances on their pay, if they were declared POWs. And the United States is not going to pay them stipends. I think that's widely supported.

Q It's not just the question of whether or not they are POWs. The Geneva Conventions provide for a review of each individual case, to determine whether that captive is POW or not. And it seems that the United States position is that the Geneva Conventions don't even apply as far as that. Why not? What is the administration's position why the Geneva Convention shouldn't apply at all?

MR. FLEISCHER: They will be treated in accordance with the principals of the Geneva Convention. There's no question about that. And the core of the Geneva Convention is focusing on humane treatment which is something the Americans have always done, and other nations around the world have not always done. We will do it because it's the right thing to do and it's the way our military treats people.

But as for the determination of whether they're POWs or not, what you have to recognize that is so different—and the President has always said this is a different kind of war, a new kind of war—is the situation surrounding the detainees in Cuba is unlike any conditions before, in previous wars, where there were simple, black and white cases of troops, typically who were drafted, who had been captured in accord with fighting for a recognized country.

That's not at all the case here. What you have here are typically non-uniformed, people who moved to Afghanistan—from more than 30 nations in the case of the detainees in Cuba—for the purpose of engaging in terror, not for the purpose of engaging in military combat, which is typically what you think of when you think of the Geneva Convention.

So as this nation, the United States, deals with a new type of war, we're also dealing with a new type of detention system — people in Cuba. And that means it's much more complicated than a simple reading of the Geneva Convention would imply. And that's why, frankly, I think it's a healthy process that's underway, where the lawyers are having a discussion about exactly how do you apply—the Geneva Convention was written in a very different era, following world war—to apply to the war on terrorism, where people don't wear uniforms, they are unlawful combatants and they come from 30 different nations, not any one recognized nation with whom the United States is fighting a war.

Q So out of that, just to nail it down, the United States is not going to provide an individual, case-by-case determination of whether or not these captives count as prisoners of war or not? We're just saying, blanket—they aren't even covered by the Geneva Convention.

MR. FLEISCHER: That issue is resolved. The issue is resolved. They are not POWs.

Q Ari, what about the Taliban fighters who were clearly fighting for their country's government? How can you not consider those as prisoners of war? And, secondly—

MR. FLEISCHER: That determination has been made. I am not an attorney and you can consult with attorneys—I know you all have and will—more specifically on the Geneva Convention. But, of course, United States never recognized the Taliban.

Q Well, what do you mean, they never—it was a government whether you recognized it or not.

MR. FLEISCHER: Well, maybe three countries in the world recognized it and, two, I'm—

Q Don't you think the United States should abide by a treaty that it signed?

MR. FLEISCHER: The United States is abiding by the core principles of that treaty.

Q What, if anything, is the administration doing to try to get this Wall Street Journal reporter out of Pakistan and what, if anything, can the administration do?

MR. FLEISCHER: In the case of Mr. Pearl, the State Department and the FBI have been in contact with the Pakistani government. He was a journalist just trying to do his job and this is a serious matter, and it is being pursued by the United States government with officials, as a reminder of the risks that journalists take, sadly, all around the world in the pursuit of journalism.

But the United States government has been in contact with the Pakistani authorities.

Q Asking them to do what and what, specifically, are we doing?

MR. FLEISCHER: Give whatever help can be given to obtain the release of him.

Q Ari, there were a lot of reports over the weekend that there was a different point of view coming out of Secretary Powell and the rest of the Cabinet. At the meeting today—I don't know if you can discuss this—but you said in the morning there was total unanimity on the issue.

MR. FLEISCHER: There is unanimity on the issue that they are not POWs. It just should go without saying that they will be treated humanely.

But there are legal issues that have been brought to the President's attention, and those are being discussed.

Q What—

MR. FLEISCHER: I am not going to describe anybody's individual conversations. This is a meeting of the NSC where the President wants to receive the counsel of all concerned, and allow them to do so privately and forthrightly.

Q POWs is now—that's it, no argument?

MR. FLEISCHER: It has not changed since David asked it to me, or Terry asked it to me or since you asked it to me. No change.

Q What was the response from the Pakistani government and what can the administration do besides ask them to help, if anything?

MR. FLEISCHER: Well, the first step is to talk to the Pakistani government, to seek their help, to try to gather whatever information is available. And that's the stage that it's at, Ron.

Q Do you know what their response was?

MR. FLEISCHER: I would leave that to the Pakistanis to describe; it's not my place.

Q Ari, there are some religious leaders who are requesting that an ecumenical delegation be allowed to visit Guantanamo. Is that something that the administration would welcome?

MR. FLEISCHER: I think that's a request that needs to be made to DOD. Those issues are not White House determinations; those are determination of the Department of Defense.

Q Two questions. One, Chairman Arafat has fired some senior member of his security force and issued arrest warrants for two others on the Palestinian Authority security force. This appears to be in response to the very strong language this weekend from the White House.

First of all, your reaction, and then I have an Afghanistan question.

MR. FLEISCHER: The reaction from the President is that it is still incumbent on Chairman Arafat to prove on a long-going, reliable and regular basis that he is determined to stop terrorism and to crack down on terrorism in the areas controlled by the Palestinian Authority in the Middle East.

And there have been arrests made before where just as soon as people were arrested, they were let out through the back door of the jail cell. So any action that could be considered progress, the President would welcome. But the burden remains on Chairman Arafat to make continued, concrete steps, so that there can be no question that Chairman Arafat is dedicated to eliminating terrorism in the region, and the President has not yet seen such steps.

Q On Afghanistan, you mentioned a moment ago, as you frequently do, that it's a different kind of war. I'm wondering if it requires a different kind of assessment of peacekeeping. Many of the independent analysts who have looked at what Afghanistan needs most the word that most often comes to their lips is security, internal security, dealing with the warlords, pacifying, even disarming them.

You made it clear this morning the United States is not going to participate in a long-term international security force. I'm wondering if you can tell us why, since so many people who look at Afghanistan's internal problems say that's what is most necessary, and if the U.S. stepped up, then the world would know that security force is real, robust and long-term?

MR. FLEISCHER: At the heart of your question is participation in the security of Afghanistan. And the answer to that is, yes, the United States will participate in helping secure the future of Afghanistan. And it's doing that through a series of ways. First and foremost is through our military presence in Afghanistan, to fight a war. The security of Afghanistan will best be obtained as a result of the United States having eliminated the al Qaeda and the Taliban, and their ability to create insecurity in Afghanistan.

Secondly, and this is something the President will address directly with Chairman Karzai at his side, the President will announce today a series of steps the United States government—the United States government will take to help secure the future of Afghanistan, through financial means, through diplomatic means, through political means. The United States has been the largest donator of food to the people of Afghanistan. We continue in that role.

When you talk about security, certainly having the people fed is part of security. And the President is very, very proud of the fact that when this war began, people were talking about widespread famine in Afghanistan. Nobody talks about that now, because the United States fed the people of Afghanistan and the United States liberated the children and the women and the hungry of Afghanistan.

So to summarize on your question, the United States is and will be dedicated to the security of Afghanistan. It will be done as a result of the war that our military fought and a result of the financial and diplomatic actions our nation will now take.

Q Does the administration accept that warlordism continues and could continue to be a problem internally, in Afghanistan with or without al Qaeda or Taliban?

MR. FLEISCHER: Sure. I mean, the history of Afghanistan for the last 20 years has been domination by a communist occupier, and then internal turmoil and chaos as a result of infiltration of Afghanistan by the al Qaeda, people who came from a different country, to prey on the

Afghani people, and warlordism, is a serious problem in Afghanistan and remains one.

Q If I can return you for a moment to the NSC meeting this morning. Set aside the POW issues, because that's not the issue under debate, The only issue under debate, as we understand it, is whether or not the Geneva Convention applies to all of these prisoners, and then you make other determinations about how you categorize.

You suggested that this was a legal issue and seemed to imply that it was an issue, therefore, that was going to be decided by lawyers. Obviously, you don't gather the President, the Vice President, the Secretary of State and others to decide an issue lawyers can decide. Who's making this decision—

MR. FLEISCHER: No, because I think it's obvious that the ramifications of legal issues can rise up to a higher level, especially when you deal with, as Helen put it, the applicability of the Geneva Convention. That's why. It's just on it's face, it rises up to the President's level.

Q So the President will make this, and he will make it with legal advice, but it's fundamentally a political decision he's going to make?

MR. FLEISCHER: No, it's a combination of legal issues that have a broader application in terms of the applicability of the Geneva Convention.

Q And did this meeting result in a resolution of that issue, not the POW issue, but that issue of the Geneva Convention?

MR. FLEISCHER: No, as I indicated, no determination has been made this morning.

Q Ari, can we come back to the Afghan peacekeeping. If every nation said that our forces are for winning wars only, not for peacekeeping, there'd be no peacekeeping forces. What exempts us?

MR. FLEISCHER: If every nation used their military forces the way the United States did, there'd be no wars.

Q Is that going to happen anytime soon?

MR. FLEISCHER: That's the point. The United States uses its military for the purpose of fighting and winning wars, which has historically resulted in more peace around the world; it has historically resulted in nations that used to be enemies becoming friends—France and Germany, for example. And that is as a result of the fact that when our nation commits its military to war, it does so for high moral purposes, backed up by military might. And the world has always been a better place for it.

Having said that, that is the contribution that this President believes should be made, by our military, to fight and win a war. And he is pleased to work with the international community on a peacekeeping mission that would focus on other nations' activities around peacekeeping. That should not be a surprise to anybody. That's exactly what the President committed to during the campaign, and that's what he intends to do.

Q Since the war and homeland defense make up a big part of the budget increase for this year, and since those needs aren't likely to diminish any time soon, does the President agree that he's become an advocate for big government in a way?

MR. FLEISCHER: No, I think the President understands that the Constitution says the first mission of the government is to provide for the common defense, and that is what the President is now faced with and that is what our nation is faced with. That's what bipartisan leaderships—congressional leadership stand so unified on, that our nation is at war. And this is a shooting war in Afghanistan. And there are moments, as the President has said, where it will be less visible. There will be moments where it is going to be more visible, and that can be anticipated into the future.

But in all cases, the first mission of any President is to make sure that our men and women who are fighting a war have the material and the ability to fight and win that war. And, secondly, to protect our homeland. What so changed for Americans on September 11th was that we were vulnerable here, within our own borders, and that's virtually without precedent in our country, certainly without modem precedent, going back to Pearl Harbor.

And on the domestic side of it, I've heard the President say this privately any number of times — and I think he's now said it publicly — the single most important thing that can be done to protect America's economy and to keep people working is to prevent another terrorist attack on America. If there was another attack anywhere along the scale of September 11th or even close to it, it could have the potential to disrupt our economy once again, not only to cost lives, but to harm the fabric of our society and our economy that keeps us strong and free.

And we are seeing increasing evidence that the recession which began some 40 days after the President took office is getting ready to turn a corner. And the President is determined to make sure it turns that corner. That's why he so strongly wants the Congress to pass a stimulus bill so we don't take any chances and leave people unemployed any longer than is ever necessary. But it's also why homeland defense is so important to protecting our security and our liberty and our economy.

Q Just to sum up, is it accurate to say that the President and Colin Powell agree on the prisoner status but may have some difference of opinion on the finer legal points? That this was hashed over in today's NSC meeting and that now the President is considering altering his view of these legal issues in response to Mr. Powell?

MR. FLEISCHER: I would simply say that the President has made no determination yet. And I did not indicate to you who was representing any point of view. As I explained earlier, that' s not my position to explain to you what any individuals say at a National Security Council meeting. I want to find that line to be helpful to you, to let you know something that took place at the NSC this morning, even though we typically do not talk about it. But I am not going to get into who said what at NSC.

Q Well, aside from the NSC meeting, is it accurate to say that Powell and the President have some difference of opinion on these finer legal points?

MR. FLEISCHER: The President always wants to encourage people in his Cabinet to come to him with their opinions and thoughts and do so in a manner that will respect their privacy, so he can get more of it.

Q Thank you.

MR. FLEISCHER: Thank you.

16

Weather and Disasters

Review Questions

1 What are some of the qualities of *USA Today*'s weather page that made it a national pacesetter?

2 When a storm strikes, readers and listeners naturally want to know whether it will be safe to travel. Stories should answer that question for readers and listeners. What other basic questions should most weather stories answer?

3 The National Weather Service is generally the most valuable source for reporters who are working on weather-related stories. List other primary sources, including several on the Internet.

4 Newspapers almost always publish year-end weather summaries. Often, these are nothing more than a mishmash of statistics. What steps can reporters take to bring these stories to life?

5 Discuss these two wire service terms:

a Bulletin

b Writethru

6 What are the essential ingredients that should be included in disaster stories?

7 Discuss the major differences between the first-day and the second-day stories on the crash of Flight 191 at Dallas-Forth Worth International Airport.

8 Discuss the pros and cons of interviewing the families of victims.

Suggested Exercises

1 Consult the Associated Press Stylebook, and define the following weather terms.

a Blizzard

b Cyclone

c Flash flood

d Flash flood warning

e Flash flood watch

f Flood

g Freeze

h Funnel cloud

i Heavy snow

j High wind

k Hurricane or typhoon

l Hurricane warning

m Ice storm, freezing drizzle, freezing rain

n Sandstorm

o Severe blizzard

p Severe thunderstorm

q Sleet

r Stockmen's advisory

s Tornado

t Travelers' advisory

u Wind chill index

v Winter storm warning

w Winter storm watch

2 Write a story based on the following information, which is from the *Hastings* (Neb.) *Tribune.*

A welcome rain was received in south central Nebraska.

The area had been suffering from drought conditions.

Rainfall amounts recorded throughout the area included Clay Center, .84; Alma, .41; Orleans, 1.10; Stamford, 1.30; Minden, 1.20; Smith Center, Kan., .75; Hebron, .70; Geneva, .47; Holdrege, 2.22; Franklin, .24.

In Hastings, the Nebraska Public Power District recorded .76 of an inch Wednesday morning; Hastings Aviation recorded .73 of an inch.

At the South Central Research and Extension Center near Clay Center, 1 inch was received. Dean Eisenhauer, irrigation specialist at the center, was quoted: "One inch is a long way from what we need, but we will take all we can get."

At any rate, the showers lifted the spirits of farmers in the area even though more moisture is needed to soak the parched land.

In fact, the executive director for the Adams County office of the federal Agricultural Stabilization and Conservation Service, Doug Carter, said of the rainfall: "It's a start. But we need 10 inches more to get back to normal."

More information from Eisenhauer: The rain will not take the pressure off of pivot irrigators. Farmers will still need to irrigate to raise soil moisture profiles before peak water usage periods in June and July.

Quotations from Eisenhauer: "It's really going to take a lot of the uncertainty out of the dryland farmer's mind. He will have a little bit more faith in his spring planting." Still, Eisenhauer noted: "The ground will still store 4 to 6 inches of moisture."

More information from Carter: Several hundred Adams County producers have applied for ASCS emergency feed programs, and he expects more producers to sign up in the following weeks. The executive director said that the drought was not over and that timely rains were still needed throughout the summer.

Carter quotation: "If we don't get timely rains, a 10-day stretch of hot-dry winds will melt a crop in a hurry."

Eugene Svoboda, a farmer in Deweese, said that the rain had helped his crops. Svoboda is a dryland farmer. He said that he would start to plant milo and feed after the rain is over. However, Svoboda said that the rain came a little late to help his winter wheat.

The Deweese farmer said that he had already pastured some of his wheat acres, and he predicted a short wheat harvest if more rain is not received. "Ten to 15 bushels per acre is going to catch it," he said.

Additional Svoboda quotation: "It makes stuff look a little better. Maybe once it breaks loose it will continue to rain."

The rains were welcome, but Franklin

County remained the driest in the area. Only .24 was received there. Lloyd Vauthrin, weather specialist in Franklin, said: "What we really need is 5 inches. The ponds are all dry, and the pasture isn't growing."

3 Write a story based on the following information, which is from the *Hastings* (Neb.) *Tribune.*

Dateline: Franklin.

Rep. Virginia Smith of Nebraska was completing a tour of southeastern Franklin County where she had met with 50 area residents who were very concerned about drought conditions.

Franklin County has had 2.31 inches of rain in the last seven months. It is May.

Earlier in the day Smith had visited a farm near Elwood. Accompanying her were Gov. Kay Orr and U.S. Agriculture Secretary Clayton Yeutter.

Franklin County was declared a disaster area last month.

During her talk to the Franklin County residents, Smith gave assurances that action is being taken to aid drought-stricken farmers. Smith told the group that Yeutter was looking into options for cattle producers.

Quotation from Smith to support her statement that Yeutter was looking into options: "He is very seriously considering opening up the CRP (Conservation Reserve Program) acres that have been seeded for two years, and have a little bit of hay on them, for haying only, not grazing."

Smith said that another option under consideration is federal assistance in transporting cattle to grazing areas or for bringing in hay.

Smith also said that she was concerned with the long-term effect the drought will have on cattle prices.

Other quotations by Smith: "I am so glad I came (to Franklin County) because I have not seen . . . anything as bad as what I have seen in the last hour. All the way as we were coming down from Gosper County it was getting worse and worse.

"I am so thankful we have a secretary of agriculture from our own state, who owns land here and who grew up here. He'll have a better understanding. (Yeutter, from Eustis, has a farm near Brady.)

"In the long term this is a disaster. We put our cattle on the market now and it's going to push the price way down and you won't get much for it, and then next year we will be short of cattle and the consumers will have to pay a whole lot more.

"Things are tough. I'm not going to be able to find all the answers to solve everything, but I am going to do the level best I can."

Quotation from Franklin Mayor Bill Nielsen, who conducted Smith's tour: "She just kept on saying that she couldn't imagine that it was this bad. It was far worse than what she had imagined it and she has seen a lot of drought areas."

4 Write a story based on the following information, which is from an Associated Press story.

A frigid air mass called the "Alberta Clipper" is moving from Canada down through the middle section of the United States.

Wind chill readings of 86 degrees below zero were recorded in North Dakota; snow totaled 15 inches in Michigan; Duluth, Minn., recorded a low of 31 degrees below zero; Embarrass, Minn., reported a low of 38 below; and, in Peoria, Ill., a reading of 13 below zero was recorded—a record for the day.

The "arctic juggernaut" roared into the nation's heartland with winds blustering to 35 mph, according to the National Weather Service.

At least four deaths were caused by the storm: three people died in traffic accidents on icy roads in Michigan, and an 18-year-old boy was found dead in Bemidji, Minn., apparently of exposure.

The National Weather Service reported that the storm's chill eventually could stretch all the way to Florida.

Harry Rixman, an official with the Florida Department of Citrus in Lakeland, was quoted: "We're going to be on our knees praying. If it gets down into the low 20s, there's not much of anything that you can do if it's for a long duration."

Florida citrus growers were using oil-burning smudge pots to help protect the trees, Rixman said.

Weather service officials in Minneapolis were warning residents not to go outside in the cold if they did not have to. At least three people were treated in Minneapolis hospitals for exposure. One was a 60-year-old man whose hands were "solidly frozen," according to Dr. Brian Mahoney of the Hennepin County Medical Center.

5 Write a forecast story based on the following information, which is from *The Arizona Republic.*

The National Weather Service is calling for mostly sunny skies and warmer temperatures for today in Phoenix. Highs will range from 80 to 85 degrees.

Low temperatures tonight should be from the mid-40s to the mid-50s.

Tomorrow is expected to be mostly sunny. Highs will be in the upper 70s and lower 80s.

Phoenix had a high temperature yesterday of 78 degrees. Also, yesterday marked the 78th consecutive day in Phoenix in which there was no precipitation.

Winds are expected to increase tomorrow in the northern mountains because of an upper-level weather disturbance, according to the National Weather Service.

The extended three-day forecast calls for partly cloudy skies. Temperatures will remain about the same.

6 Write a story based on the following information, which is from *The Beaumont* (Texas) *Enterprise.*

Beaumont schools remained open despite icy highways in southeast Texas, but hazardous road conditions forced closings in nearby counties.

Temperatures dropped to 31 degrees in the early-morning hours. Temperatures climbed only five degrees above that the rest of the day.

Minor accidents were reported throughout the area. Cars reportedly slid off highways throughout southeast Texas. None of the accidents, however, caused serious injuries.

The Golden Triangle [the area in which Beaumont is located] remained virtually ice free until late Friday [the day before publication]. East Texas counties reported roads that were glazed with ice. Sleet fell most of Friday.

Sections of Interstate 10 in Louisiana were closed much of Friday.

A Department of Public Safety spokeswoman said Friday afternoon that travel conditions around Houston were extremely hazardous.

Officials in Nacogdoches and Angelina counties told the *Enterprise* that a downpour of sleet had forced road closings there. Loop 69 North around Lufkin was closed by 6 p.m.

Roads were still open in Jasper County, but officials said that they anticipated closing the hilly sections of U.S. 96 as the road conditions continued to deteriorate throughout Friday. Deputy Sheriff Joe Thornton was the source of the information.

Thornton also said: "Troopers are going a maximum speed of 25 to 30 mph on their way to accidents. The road conditions are bad."

An 18-wheeler skidded on an ice-covered bridge on Interstate 10 in Chambers County. It blocked traffic on the Farm Road 146 overpass late Thursday for more than an hour.

The Department of Public Safety reported ice building up on bridges in Orange County late Friday. It was also accumulating on highways and roads. Freezing drizzle, temperatures hovering around 30 degrees and high winds were also reported late Friday. Sand was being placed on bridges throughout Friday night.

7 Write a story based on the following information, which is from *The Gleaner* in Henderson, Ky.

Snow should total between 1 and 3 inches in Henderson today [Saturday], according to Francis Burns, a National Weather Service forecaster in Evansville, Ind. There is a 60 percent chance of snow on Sunday, with the potential of leaving up to 3 more inches.

Henderson is on the northern fringe of a winter storm that is moving south.

Blowing and drifting snow was reported. There were also winter storm warnings and slow-moving traffic in Henderson. The National Weather Service in Evansville said that the weather could get worse.

Portions of eastern Kentucky could possibly receive 6 inches of snow. But, according to Burns, the Henderson area would not receive that much.

Burns was quoted: "This one (the storm) on Sunday has the potential to move farther north. We'll be more specific as time goes on."

The high in Henderson was expected to reach about 20 degrees, according to Burns. Winds were forecast to be out of the north at between 10 and 15 mph. The overnight low was forecast to be about 10 degrees.

Snow is in the extended forecast, according to Burns. It is too early to tell for sure, but Burns said that a chance of a light snow had been predicted for Tuesday and Wednesday.

Approximately 2 inches of snow fell on Henderson Thursday night. That added to the 1 inch that was already on the ground.

The threat of more bad weather led to a minor run on area grocery stores.

Cars jammed the parking lot and fire lanes at the Sureway store in Eastgate late Friday afternoon. Shoppers had to wait in line just for grocery carts. Each check-out station was stacked 12 people deep.

Marvin Hancock, store manager, said: "It's been like this all day."

Hancock said that the large crowds were a "combination of Friday, the first of the month and the snow. With all that, you've got a madhouse."

He continued: "People have really taken the situation well, as far as waiting to get checked out. When they see you have all your lanes open and all your people up front, they know you're trying."

Store manager Bud Satterfield also reported a bustling business at the Dix Gold Star Foods store at the U.S. 42-North store.

Satterfield said that the store had sold out of bread but that milk remained.

Area roads remained covered with snow and ice. Road crews were out trying to stay ahead of the predicted storms.

8 When a powerful earthquake rocked northern California, reporters from throughout the world focused on San Francisco, Oakland and other cities. It was a major disaster and a major story. The initial casualty counts and damage estimates were inaccurate, but reporters could go only with the information they had as the story was breaking. Your assignment is to write a breaking story based on the following information, which is from an Associated Press story. Your deadline is 8 p.m., about three hours after the earthquake struck.

Game No. 3 of the World Series between the San Francisco Giants and the Oakland Athletics was scheduled to start at 5:31 p.m. on Tuesday.

At 5:04 p.m. the quake struck.

Tom Mullins, spokesman for the California Office of Emergency Services, said that preliminary figures indicated at least 400 people had been injured throughout the area.

Officials are saying that at least 215 people were killed. That included at least 200 people who were crushed to death in their cars when a mile-long section of Interstate 880 in Oakland collapsed onto the lower level.

A section of the San Francisco-Oakland Bay Bridge also collapsed. There was widespread damage to buildings, and fires were ignited by the quake.

Marty Boyer, public information officer for Alameda County, is the person who estimated that at least 200 people were killed in the Interstate 880 collapse.

The quake registered 6.9 on the Richter scale and was on the notorious San Andreas Fault.

There were 60,000 fans at Candlestick Park in San Francisco awaiting the start of the World Series game. They had to be evacuated.

No serious injuries were reported at the stadium.

San Francisco Mayor Art Agnos talked to you and to other reporters. He said that eight people were killed in San Francisco. Five of them were killed when buildings collapsed on cars. Three died in a fire in the Marina section of the city. The Marina blaze was still burning at 8 p.m.

There were no reports of major damage in high-rise buildings.

Eileen Mahoney, Agnos' press secretary, said that 20 people were injured in the Marina fire.

Here is what was happening in some other cities:

A fire was blazing near downtown Berkeley.

Six people were killed in the collapse of part of the City Garden Mall in Santa Cruz. That's according to the California Highway Patrol.

One person died of a heart attack and four people were injured in San Jose, which is 50 miles south of San Francisco. That's according to Willis Jacobs at the National Earthquake Information Center in Golden, Colo.

The 6.9 Richter reading made this the sixth-most-powerful quake to strike California this century. It was the most powerful quake since 1980, when a 7.0 quake was centered in Eureka.

On the basis of the fatality reports you have so far, this quake was the deadliest to hit California since a 6.6 tremor killed 65 people in the San Fernando Valley of southern California on Feb. 9, 1971. That quake did severe damage, too.

As night fell in San Francisco, thousands of office workers, who had no transportation home, mingled with homeless people downtown.

Fire and ambulance sirens howled.

Here are some quotations from people you were able to interview.

Greg Higgins, who was driving north in Watsonville near Santa Cruz when the quake struck: "You could see dozens of huge booms of smoke going into the air. It looked like bombs going off into the city . . . it was complete pandemonium. There were three major fires near us. There was no power in the city at all."

Jeannine Marchanks, who was at the San Francisco Airport when the quake struck: "It was horrible. It got gradually bigger and bigger. Windows started rattling. Things were falling from the ceiling."

In San Francisco, electrically powered trolleys formed little empty holes of light where they stalled, emergency blinkers winking in and out. Car headlights crisscrossed, and pedestrians dodged among them.

People gathered in candle-lit bars and restaurants. On sidewalks downtown, groups of 10 or 20 people stood, listening on large radios to reports of the earthquake.

Buses were jammed, but no one appeared to panic.

17

Broadcast Writing

Review Questions

1 Define the following terms.

a Anchor

b Actuality

c Lead-in

d Wrap

e Throw line

f Wind-up line

2 Summarize the evolution of broadcast writing style.

3 List five guidelines to follow when presenting numerical information.

4 List four guidelines to follow when making time references.

5 List four guidelines to follow when using titles.

6 What is the primary guideline to remember when using abbreviations?

7 List three guidelines for sentence structure when writing for broadcast.

8 List and discuss Professor Ben Silver's, Wendy Black's and Professor Dave Ogden's suggestions for students who aspire to positions in broadcast journalism.

9 Discuss the art of "storytelling" as it applies to broadcast news writing and reporting.

Suggested Exercises

1 Edit the following sentences for broadcast style.

a VOTERS APPROVED A $13.5 MILLION BOND ISSUE BY A 4-1 MARGIN.

b 2.1% OF THE DISTRICT'S 99,985 REGISTERED VOTERS CAST BALLOTS.

c THE ISSUE WAS APPROVED AT ALL 11 OF THE DISTRICT'S POLLING SITES.

d ABOUT 35,000 WORKERS ARE EXPECTED TO STRIKE.

e THE DEFICIT IS EXPECTED TO BE $5,050,000.85.

f ONLY ABOUT 1/8 OF THE REGISTERED VOTERS CAST BALLOTS.

g THE REGISTRATION FEE FOR THE SUMMER PROGRAM WILL BE $35.50.

h WILLARD JOHNSON, 82, A STATE SENATOR, DIED FRIDAY.

i NEARLY 1,000,000 FARMERS ARE HAVING FINANCIAL DIFFICULTIES.

j "I EXPECT THE PRESIDENT TO VETO THE BILL," THE SENATOR SAID.

k CHARLES DARLINGTON, A STATE REPRESENTATIVE FROM NUCKOLLS COUNTY, WAS ELECTED SPEAKER OF THE HOUSE.

l THE NATIVE OF LINCOLN, NEB., IS THE FEATURED SPEAKER.

m HE WAS REPRESENTED BY AN ACLU ATTORNEY.

n JOHN SMITH, A 36-YEAR-OLD UNEMPLOYED ROOFER WITH A HISTORY OF SEX-CRIME CONVICTIONS, WAS CHARGED WITH RAPE TODAY IN COUNTY COURT.

o JOHNSON WAS THE TEAM'S LEADING SCORER WITH TWENTY-THREE POINTS.

2 The following story was transmitted on The Associated Press newspaper wire. Rewrite it for broadcast.

CRABB, Texas (AP)—Voters in this farming community Saturday overwhelmingly rejected a plan to incorporate, a move the town's 12-year-old mayor had sought to prevent annexation by neighboring cities.

"It's back to the drawing board," a frowning Mayor Brian Zimmerman said after the 595-30 vote against incorporation, which also allowed him to keep his job.

Only 33 percent of 1,911 eligible voters cast ballots, and Zimmerman wasn't among them because of his age.

Although failing in his campaign promise of incorporation, Zimmerman gets to retain his title as mayor. He said he doesn't plan to give up on incorporation.

When Zimmerman, then 11, was elected mayor in an unofficial election in September, he vowed to put Crabb on the map by seeking incorporation.

Incorporation, he said, would prevent adjacent cities such as Richmond, Rosenberg and especially Houston from annexing it. Crabb is about 20 miles south of Houston.

3 The following story was transmitted on The Associated Press newspaper wire. Rewrite it for broadcast.

ST. PAUL, Minn. (AP)—State revenue collections still show a deficit that will wipe out the $450 million "rainy day" fund by the end of the current two-year budget period, legislators have been told.

A memorandum prepared by Senate researchers said revenues for July, August and September—the first quarter of the new fiscal year—are running "slightly ahead of expectations."

The expectations, however, were for a shortfall that would use up the rainy day fund created as a cushion for the state budget.

The research report to members of the Senate on Tuesday said that, if the present pattern continues, the $450 million budget reserve will be drawn down with the budget near balance at the end of the biennium.

Finance Commissioner Jay Kiedrowski called the conclusions "premature."

Kiedrowski said his department will have new projections of state finances Oct. 22 for the second quarter of the new fiscal year.

Kiedrowski said there is a possibility that the new forecast will use different figures from those the state has been working on since spring. Instead of making a single budget forecast, Kiedrowski has predicted possible shortfalls of $134 million, $533 million or $811 million, depending upon economic conditions.

Those figures "may be altered in the new forecast to reflect changing situations," he said Tuesday.

State revenues were slightly ahead of expectations in July but dipped in August.

4 The following story was transmitted on The Associated Press newspaper wire. Rewrite it for broadcast.

BLOOMINGTON, Minn. (AP) — Triple Five Corp., the City Council and the Bloomington Port Authority have signed a development agreement for the proposed mega-mall that puts final action on the proposed $1.5 billion facility one step closer to reality.

The last major stumbling block has been approval of a package of tax breaks by the state Legislature—an action legislative leaders said likely won't be discussed until next year.

The agreement signed Monday would allow the terms to end if lawmakers cannot reach agreement by Nov. 1 on a funding proposal that would provide the developer $15 million in subsidies for the next 24 years.

The Nov. 1 deadline is unrealistic, legislative leaders have said, and Bloomington Mayor James Lindau has said it may not be absolute. But he insists that unless the Legislature acts by year's end, the mega-mall will be dead.

The Port Authority's vote for the agreement was unanimous; the City Council's vote was 6–1.

The one "no" vote was cast by council member Neil Peterson, who said he fears the mall could change the "demeanor" of Bloomington into something more akin to Las Vegas.

The mega-mall proposal is "like having a gorilla in your back yard," he said. "How do you feed it after it grows up?"

According to the agreement, if Triple Five abandons the project before construction starts, the city is entitled to $5.5 million in damages. Additionally, the property at the old Met Stadium site reverts to city ownership if construction does not go forward.

As soon as the Legislature approves what the agreement calls a "state participation package," Triple Five is required to provide a $2 million letter of credit.

The city is counting on the revenue from a lodging and liquor tax in the city, an exemption from the metrowide tax-base sharing pool for the mega-mall site and the dedication of one-sixth of the 6 percent sales tax collected on retail sales at the mega-mall, said Bloomington finance officer Lyle Olson.

5 The following story was transmitted on The Associated Press newspaper wire. Rewrite it for broadcast.

AUSTIN, Minn. (AP)—A federal mediation session has been scheduled for Monday in the seven-week-old strike by union meatpackers at the Geo. A. Hormel & Co. plant.

It's the first time the two sides have met since some 1,500 members of Local P-9 of the United Food and Commercial Workers union struck the Austin plant on Aug. 17 in a dispute over wages and benefits.

Federal mediator Hank Bell set the meeting, but the location was not announced.

Bell has said he had been trying to arrange a meeting before a request last week from Gov. Rudy Perpich to the Federal Mediation and Conciliation Service in Minneapolis to resume the talks.

6 Here is the information from a broadcast wire story transmitted by the Minneapolis bureau of The Associated Press. Write a broadcast story based on the information.

Bobbi Polzine (pohl-zeen′) and her husband, Alfred, who farm 400 acres near Brewster, Minn., have dug a ditch across their driveway and barricaded the farm to thwart any repossession attempt.

Bobbi Polzine is co-founder of the farm activist group "Groundswell."

A judge yesterday signed an order that authorizes the Worthington, Minn., Production Credit Association to repossess the Polzines' livestock and machinery in order to satisfy a debt.

Doug McCool, the head of the farm credit services in Worthington, confirmed that negotiations between his organization, the Polzines and their attorney took place last night and will continue today. The negotiations center on whether the Polzines could keep operating their farm.

McCool said: "I believe we are very close to an agreement that would be in the best financial interest of all parties."

The negotiations have helped to avert a confrontation at the southwestern Minnesota farm.

Nobles County Sheriff Dale Peters said that he was thinking about going on vacation to give the parties time to come up with a compromise.

Peters said that he wanted no violence at the Polzines' farm. He said: "We aren't living in different countries where we have to hold hostages."

An announcement could come today on the outcome of the negotiations.

7 Here is the information from a broadcast wire story transmitted by the Minneapolis bureau of The Associated Press. Write a broadcast story based on the information.

A rally was held last night at the Benson High School Gymnasium in Benson, Minn.

About 900 farmers and businesspeople attended.

Gov. Rudy Perpich spoke to the group. He said: "I can assure you I will not sit by and let our farm families get wiped out in Minnesota. It might happen in other states, but it won't happen in Minnesota."

Agriculture Commissioner Jim Nichols also spoke.

Independent state Sen. Charlie Berg from Chokio (shuh-ky′ oh) said that a large part of rural America is approaching insolvency.

Berg said that farm prices are 20 percent lower this year than last year, and farmers will pay $1 billion more in expenses this year than they get in income.

Berg said: "We need a price. There's no other solution."

Gov. Perpich said that he will lobby Congress to pass the farm bill sponsored by Iowa Sen. Tom Harkin.

Nichols said that Harkin's bill will satisfy three criteria needed to help farmers: it will double farm income, cut taxpayers' costs and increase exports in both dollars and bushels.

8 Here is the information from a story written by Mike Sauceda, a reporter for KOOL radio in Phoenix. Write a broadcast story based on the information.

The temperature hit 100 degrees for the first time this year at 12:46 p.m., today (May 2).

According to Craig Ellis of the National Weather Service in Phoenix, the earliest 100-degree reading for the city occurred on April 14, 1925, 1959 and 1985.

Here is an eight-second actuality from Ellis: "The chance of getting 100 degrees this early in the season is about 20 percent, or actually a little less than 20 percent."

9 Here is information from a story written by Mark Carlson, a reporter for KOOL radio in Phoenix. Write a broadcast story based on the information.

A family planning bill passed the Arizona House but was killed a few minutes later in the Senate because Democrats were upset that moderate Republicans attempted to compromise with anti-abortionists.

The bill would have allocated $300,000 for planning services for poor people. The bill stipulated that money would go to counties, not to private agencies such as Planned Parenthood.

Rep. Trent Franks of Phoenix noted that improvements were made in the bill. But he still cast a nay vote in the House.

Here is a 15-second actuality from Franks: "I have to vote no on the bill because some of the funds can still be used for abortion counseling. But it'll certainly be a lot less than it was before. I appreciate everyone trying to make it better."

Part Five

Beats

18

Multicultural Reporting

Review Questions

1 The demographics of the United States—its density, its distribution and the composition of its population—are changing. Discuss the challenges this presents to the media.

2 What were some of the primary findings and conclusions of the 1968 report issued by the National Advisory Commission on Civil Disorders, a group most commonly referred to as the Kerner Commission?

a

b

c

3 The American Society of Newspaper Editors (ASNE) conducts an annual census to determine the number of minority journalists who work in the country's newsrooms. What was the primary finding of the 2001 census?

4 The textbook chapter discusses a major four-part series by the media critic of the *Los Angeles Times,* David Shaw, that examined multiculturalism in American newsrooms. What were some of the most common criticisms of the media that Shaw noted?

a

b

c

d

e

5 List and discuss the guidelines the textbook chapter provides for improving minority affairs reporting.

a

b

c

d

e

f

g

h

i

6 The textbook chapter reprints a checklist for improving news coverage of minority affairs. That checklist was distributed at the seminar on "Riot and Reconstruction: Covering the Continuing Story," which was held shortly after the 1992 Los Angeles uprising that followed the verdict in the Rodney King case. List the items on the checklist that were adapted from recommendations of *The Seattle Times'* Racial Awareness Pilot Project; Sandy Rivera, KHOU-TV, Houston; Sherrie Mazingo, a University of Southern California journalism professor; and Mervin Aubespin of *The Courier-Journal* in Louisville, Ky.

a

b

c

d

e

f

g

h

i

j

k

l

7 Discuss Associated Press style on:

a Use of the word *African*

b Use of the word *black*

c Use of the word *Canuck*

d Use of the word *colored*

e Use of the word *honky*

Suggested Exercises

1 Clip five stories from newspapers or magazines that provide coverage of minority groups or issues. Analyze and evaluate the stories. For example: Is there evidence of stereotyping? Have unrepresentative minority "spokespersons" been relied upon? Has insensitive language been used?

2 Determine the demographics of your geographical area and compare them with the demographics of the staffs of newspaper and television newsrooms in your region.

3 Here is information from a story written by Dawn Garcia for the *San Francisco Chronicle.* Write a story based on the information.

A study was released by the Coalition for Immigrant and Refugee Rights and Services. The study was conducted over a period of seven months; it was one of the first of its kind in the nation.

The study focused on undocumented women immigrants in the Bay Area who lived in San Francisco, Alameda and San Mateo counties.

Most previous studies that focused on undocumented immigrants have centered on families or men. Women in most previous studies have been seen simply as "appendages" of the men they immigrated with, according to Karen Rosen, one of the study's authors.

The study noted, however, that women make up more than half of all undocumented immigrants now in the United States.

The study, which was based on interviews with more than 400 Bay Area women from Latin America, the Philippines, China and Hong Kong, produced these findings:

1. Some 64 percent of the Latinas and 57 percent of the Filipinas surveyed said they feared deportation and thus they avoided using public services such as medical care or welfare. Interestingly, some of the women said they fear even leaving the house to get items such as groceries.

2. Some two in five Latinas in the study said they came to the Bay Area by themselves; 23 percent said they brought children with them.

3. Nine percent of the Latinas interviewed had graduated from high school; 77 percent of the Filipinas had graduated. Twenty-nine percent of the Filipinas also had a college degree.

The authors of the study said they were alarmed at the findings. They said that the results show that the children of the women, many of them born U.S. citizens, are in jeopardy.

The study also found that the undocumented women immigrants in the Bay Area are a growing and neglected population.

Some direct quotes:

From Leni Marin, who heads the San Francisco Commission on the Status of Women: "Our misconceptions and ignorance about the life experiences, the hopes and the dreams of undocumented women have been challenged by this report."

From Chris Hogeland, co-author of the study: "One woman we talked to, typical of many, was afraid to go to (San Francisco) General Hospital because she thought the hospital would immediately call the INS (U.S. Immigration and Naturalization Service) and deport her."

19

City Government

Review Questions

1 Discuss the following forms of government.

a Mayor-council

b Council-manager

c Commission

2 What is an agenda for a city council meeting? Discuss why it is important for reporters to review agendas before meetings.

3 What is an executive session?

4 List the 15 techniques for covering public meetings that were compiled at the *Daily Hampshire Gazette,* Northampton, Mass.

a

b

c

d

e

f

g

h

i

j

k

l

m

n

o

5 List the nine steps that lead to passage of the city budget in Tempe, Ariz. (These steps vary slightly in different communities, but the process in Tempe is representative.)

a

b

c

d

e

f

g

h

i

6 Discuss the following.

a Capital budget

b Operating budget

c Mill levy

7 List the basic information that should be included in most budget stories.

a

b

c

d

e

f

g

8 Figures in budget stories can be intimidating to reporters and readers. What writing approaches can reporters use to make budget stories understandable to readers?

9 List and discuss 11 tips for covering local government.

a

b

c

d

e

f

g

h

i

j

k

Suggested Exercises

1 Write a news story based on the following information, which is from an article in *The Birmingham* (Ala.) *News.*

Dateline—MONTGOMERY.

The results of a statewide survey, conducted by 2,221 educators and community leaders, were released Monday.

According to Superintendent of Education Wayne Teague, Alabama school systems need to hire 7,900 additional professional and support staff employees. The cost would be $251 million.

The assessment team suggested hiring more than 2,300 elementary school teachers at a cost of $86 million; 644 junior high teachers at a cost of $24 million; more than 1,000 high school teachers at a cost of $37 million; more than 760 special-education instructors at a cost of $28 million; almost 1,400 administrators and supervisors at a cost of $51 million; and almost 1,800 support personnel at a cost of $25 million.

Teague said that a dire personnel shortage exists in Alabama city and county school systems. He said that if the problem continues to go unattended, it could threaten the state's future economic and social well being.

Teague also said that he did not expect any major changes in the way the state funds education until after the next elections. He said that he agreed with U.S. Sen. Richard Shelby's comments at the Alabama Education Association state convention in Montgomery last week. Shelby said that the state must invest in education if it hopes to move ahead.

Teague also noted that the "climate" is not right for tax reform now.

Quotations from Teague: "You might see some tokenism, but nothing significant, before the elections.... It is very obvious that many, if not all, of our city and county systems are facing a dire personnel shortage. If we are to continue to make further improvements in the years ahead, there must be a restructuring of the way we finance elementary and secondary schools. We cannot make the kind of progress we need to make in our school systems by counting solely on just the growth in the Special Education Trust Fund."

Teague also noted that: "Two of the greatest needs are guidance counselors and special-education teachers."

2 Write a news story based on the following information, which is from an article in the *Hastings* (Neb.) *Tribune.*

An architectural firm, Berggren and Woll, and Fred Thompson and Associates, an engineering firm, both of Lincoln, conducted an energy audit of the Adams County Courthouse. The Adams County Board of Supervisors had approved the $2,500 audit in October.

Representatives of the two firms reported back to the Board of Supervisors on Tuesday.

On the basis of a physical examination of the building and information provided by blueprints and custodian Marvin Hartman, the firms recommended six energy conservation plans that they said could save Adams County more than $55,000 each year.

The board members, after hearing the report, generally agreed that most of the recommendations warranted further study.

The recommendations:

The county could meter water that does not go into the city's sanitary sewer separately to reduce the county's sewer fee. Annual energy cost savings is estimated at $9,000, with a six-month payback on the costs of the meters.

The county could install a separate heating and air-conditioning system in the sheriff's office. Costs would then be reduced by shutting off the main system in the courthouse on weekends and holidays. Annual savings is estimated at $13,000, with a 1½-year payback on an estimated initial cost of $15,500.

The county could install variable volume fans to reduce energy requirements of fans that currently move more air than needed for the heating and air-conditioning systems. Annual savings is estimated at $9,000, with a 4½-year payback on an estimated initial cost of $40,800.

The county could install inside glass panels on the existing glass to reduce heating and air-conditioning losses. Annual energy cost savings is $6,000, with a 12-year payback based on an initial cost of $75,000.

The county could install new dampers. Annual energy cost savings is estimated at $550, with a 2½-year payback on an initial investment of $1,200.

The county could replace pre-cooling coils in the air-conditioning system. This would result in an estimated annual cost savings of $1,300, with a 10-year payback on an initial cost of $12,600.

Quotation from Supervisor Lavern Mosier: "It's something that has to be done in due time. If kept up-to-date, we will have a useful building."

3 Write a news story based on the following information, which is from an article in *The Birmingham* (Ala.) *News.*

Texas Education Corp. bought Southern Technical College in Birmingham last July.

The private trade school lost $235,000 last year and $62,000 in January, according to budget statements the Texas Education Corp. supplied to union negotiators.

At present, the school is deadlocked in pay negotiations with the Retail, Wholesale, Department Store, Services Union that instructors voted to join last December.

Chris House, faculty representative for Southern Technical College, said that the American Federation of Teachers recommended the union as an aggressive one that could carry the trade school instructors through a long legal battle.

The latest belt-tightening measure came last week when the school slashed its instructors' pay. Faculty warned that the cut undermines the education provided to students.

The cut—15 percent—will force out experienced instructors who can be replaced with cheaper—but less qualified—newcomers, according to House. The cut sliced House's earnings to less than $9 an hour.

House also contended that the Texas Education Corp. has already fired several experienced instructors to help balance the books of the financially troubled operation. House also said that the company is forcing remaining instructors to teach an excessive number of classes, some of which they are not qualified to teach.

Wayne Apostolico, director of operations for Texas Education, said that the school was not seeking less costly replacements for more experienced faculty and that it was merely trying to straighten out the school's finances. He denied that some classes had unqualified instructors.

Apostolico noted that the school had 163 students, too few to support so many instructors. He said that the school now has 12 full-time and part-time instructors. He also said that the school is starting courses that will attract more students.

Apostolico agreed that some instructors taught a wide variety of courses. But he said this did not detract from the educational mission. He noted that computer-aided drafting instructors, for example, were qualified to teach typing since they used a keyboard.

Apostolico blamed union activities for disrupting the educational atmosphere. He said that he would not discuss the school's finances except to say that the company had no plans to close the school.

Quotation from Apostolico: "It's our intention to provide a good, quality education. We recognize as a company that if we don't place students, we'll go out of business."

Quotation from House: "Instructors can't stay long for that kind of money (as reflected by the cuts). The company will probably make the school profitable. I don't know if they'll make it sound educationally.

"There is a lot of pressure to teach classes you don't think you're qualified for. You can either teach them or leave, and a lot of times you can't afford to leave."

Ruffus Hartley, 58, said that he has taught board drafting for 15 years. He took his last typing classes in the 1940s, but was forced to teach typing.

House said that Hartley didn't even know how to turn on the electric typewriters.

Quotation from Hartley: "I certainly was not qualified to teach typing." Hartley was dismissed last fall.

4 Write a news story based on the following information, which is from an article in the *Star-Herald* of Scottsbluff, Neb.:

LB 662 was scheduled for first-round debate today in the Nebraska Legislature by special order of Speaker William Nichol of Scottsbluff.

The bill would require the state's 650-plus Class I school districts to consolidate with larger districts. Class I districts offer classes only through the eighth grade. Class III districts offer classes in kindergarten through high school.

Sponsors of the bill are Dave Landis of Lincoln, Vard Johnson of Omaha and Peter Hoagland of Omaha. They contend that the reorganization would provide a more equitable tax base. The bill is also supported by the Nebraska Association of School Boards, which generally favors consolidation.

Proponents of the bill say that Class I districts tend to have lower tax levies.

Sue Ewing, a board member of the Cedar Canyon Class I district southwest of Gering [and in the *Star-Herald's* circulation area], and other Nebraska Panhandle residents joined an estimated 300 opponents of the bill, who journeyed to Lincoln [the state capital] hoping to influence senators last week.

Today's vote will determine whether the effort won any senators over.

Mrs. Ewing and other opponents of the bill contend that it will not lower property taxes as promised.

Mrs. Ewing said that in Scotts Bluff [two words] County, the average levy for Class I districts is about $1.90 per $100 valuation. School taxes in Class III districts average about $2.40 per $100.

Mrs. Ewing was quoted: "It looks on the surface that Class I's get a real tax break," she said. "But the real bottom line is dollars per household."

According to Mrs. Ewing, the average taxpayer in a Class I district in Scotts Bluff County pays $2,274 in educational taxes compared with $1,288 for taxpayers in Class III districts.

She said: "We tend to have more valuation with fewer kids." It was also noted that the disparity includes non-resident tuition, which Class I residents pay to send high school students to Class III districts.

The bill would allow Class III school boards to maintain smaller schools. But few opponents believe this would actually happen. Mrs. Ewing quoted some of the bill's opponents who lived in districts that had already been absorbed by larger districts. She said they told her that they got "shabby treatment—they were sent the most untrained teachers, the oldest books."

Other area residents who went to Lincoln last week were Cedar Canyon board president Russ Worthman and member Gary Grasmick, Lake Alice board member Jim Merrigan and Jack Preston, a past president of the Rural School Board Association.

Mrs. Ewing was further quoted: "If you lose your local control, you might as well close the school. There were probably 300 rural patrons roaming the [state capitol] halls. I hope we did some good. We won't know till they [the senators] push the buttons [to vote]."

5 Write a news story based on the following information, which is from an article in the *Colorado Springs* (Colo.) *Gazette Telegraph* (assume that you are writing for a Tuesday morning edition in January).

Colorado Springs will begin the process of selecting a replacement for current City Manager George Fellows by advertising the position with organizations for municipal officials in early February. Hundreds of applications are expected.

A successor to Fellows is expected on the job no later than July 1.

Fellows recently announced that he will leave his post of 18 years on June 30 and will take vacation time until retirement in September. He will turn 65 in September.

Fellows, Mayor Bob Isaac and Personnel Director Dick Zickefoose developed a procedure that would have created a council committee of three—two incumbents and one newly elected in April—to have much of the power for a selection.

The committee was to have been appointed after April's election of four council members. It would have screened applications and interviewed four to six of the best candidates. The entire council would then have interviewed only two or three finalists before making a selection.

Monday the City Council agreed that the screening committee will instead recommend up to 20 names to the full council. The council would then decide how many people to interview. The entire council would then interview all finalists.

The broader responsibility for the entire council was recommended by members Kathy Loo, Buster Cogswell, Dave Sarton and Mary Vieth. All others agreed. Thus, the full council will be more involved in selecting a new city manager than city administrators originally recommended.

Cogswell said that each member should be able to screen all résumés. He also contended that any council member should be able to recommend any applicant for an interview.

Cogswell was quoted: "Every council member owes that responsibility to the electorate."

Councilman Bill Snyder asked Zickefoose what the salary range for a city manager would be. Zickefoose said that the range would be advertised with a note that the normal appointment would be at the midpoint of the range. The range for this year's city manager is $66,336 to $99,504 a year.

Fellows' current salary is $81,013.

Snyder said that he did not want Fellows' current salary to be advertised. He was quoted as saying: "That could cause problems." Councilman Frank Parisi agreed that it could cause problems.

The council agreed Monday that the screening committee would select the best candidates between April 15 and 30. It would then recommend that group to the council. The council would do interviewing May 1–15 and would make an offer by May 15 to its choice.

The person who accepts the job would be expected to report for work between June 15 and July 1.

The City Charter gives the city manager final responsibility for nearly all administrative matters. These include running the large city-owned utilities and general city departments. The person also has hiring and firing authority over nearly all the city's 3,200 employees.

6 Write a news story based on the following information, which is from an article in *The Beaumont* (Texas) *Enterprise* (assume that you are writing the article for a March edition).

Louise Crew, a retired nurse and teacher from Orange, Texas, was selected to be a Senior Legislative Intern.

She was the only Orange County person selected for the honor.

State Sen. Carl Parker started the Senior Legislative Intern program in 1978. It is based upon nominations.

Parker chose the group for the first year. Since then, each year's interns have chosen their own successors from applications.

Parker greeted Mrs. Crew and provided a daily program of legislative meetings and a tour.

Mrs. Crew is a great-grandmother. She promotes community flag-flying each Fourth of July. She was the first Senior Legislative Intern of the current legislative session in Austin.

She was quoted:

"The most interesting part was sitting in on committee meetings, hearing them discuss the pros and cons of bills coming up—and seeing how much discussion goes on before they are taken up as bills by the Legislature.

"What I plan to do now is share information with senior groups in the district. The more they are informed, the better they are able to influence the Legislature in doing what we want done.

"The only way the Legislature knows our feelings is for us to tell them."

Mrs. Crew spent a week in February at the Capitol. Parker chairs the Educational Committee. Mrs. Crew's daughter, Ann Palmer, who is interested in education, accompanied her to the Capitol.

Mrs. Crew said that Parker was "a very charming man, very popular among senators." Parker gave Mrs. Crew, at his own expense, a flag flown over the Capitol.

Mrs. Crew likes to relax with needlework and crafts. She enjoys quilting. She has won awards for her quilts and crafts at Senior Citizens Rally Days. She is also involved in community activities.

District 4 Senior Legislative Interns who will follow Mrs. Crew during the 69th Legislative session are Alfred Valdez and Juanita Whitley of Port Arthur, Thomas James Smith of Nederland, Katherine S. Enloe of Cleveland and Elmer W. Wadleigh, Bessie Whitney and Thelma P. Williams of Beaumont.

Mrs. Crew earned her LVN at Lamar University in 1953 and spent 16 years nursing. Of the 16 years, she spent 13 as owner of the 25-bed White Oak Nursing Home in Mauriceville.

She followed her mother into the teaching profession and taught before going into nursing. Mrs. Crew taught the combined primary grades (first through third) in a McLewis county school, where she was one of two teachers. She also taught at Magnolia Grove Elementary School in Vidor.

Mrs. Crew was quoted:

"I was teaching on my 16th birthday. That was so long ago, I can hardly remember. Back then, when you married you stopped teaching."

During her week in Austin, she was busy. It was Port Arthur Day during the week, and so she attended the Cajun Day Festival. She also met state Rep. Ron Lewis. Lewis introduced her to a member of the Committee on Aging. Mrs. Crew learned the status of Retired Senior Volunteer Program (R.S.V.P.) and nutrition programs. Concerning this, she was quoted: "Both (programs) have been allocated increased funding due to depressed economic conditions in the district."

She also attended lengthy meetings of the Finance and the Jurisprudence committees and an Intergovernmental Relations Committee hearing. In addition, she attended a meeting of the Texas Agency on Aging and heard discussion on hunger, housing and community-based care for the elderly.

Mrs. Crew is very interested in quality of life for the elderly. She is active as a volunteer with R.S.V.P. She does grocery shopping for homebound older persons. She has been recognized for the amount of hours contributed. She also works in the pantry of First Baptist Church. She screens applicants to determine need. She also serves on the ACTION committee [A Commitment to Improve Orange Now]. She is a member of Heritage House Museum and American Association of Retired People.

Here is another quotation by Mrs. Crew:

"Sen. Parker instigated R.S.V.P. to keep older people active, and to find out their needs. Parker was instrumental in getting R.S.V.P. into a bill—and it grew out of that. Now the federal government puts in money and pays coordinators."

7 Write a news story for a Wednesday edition based on the following information, which is from an article in *The Gleaner* in Henderson, Ky.

A public hearing was held Tuesday night to consider a $24.6 million stormwater management plan prepared by an engineering consultant.

Several members of the audience questioned parts of the plan presented by Zack Fuller of Proctor-Davis-Ray Engineers. But no outright opposition surfaced.

The mayor and several commissioners spoke and said that they are convinced that some action is needed to prevent damage and inconvenience caused by periodic flooding in several sections of the city.

The city officials promised at the public

hearing to explore every possibility to minimize the financial impact of any plan. The officials said that citizens will be given ample opportunity to voice their views.

Mayor William Newman told the 20 persons who attended the session: "We're not naive enough to believe we can do all of these things."

Cost figures discussed at the public hearing were somewhat lower than those discussed at a Monday night work session, apparently because they were more precise.

Retiree Paul Gorby criticized Fuller for presenting three potential methods for financing. He said: "It looks to me like the committee did away with the other two methods" in favor of a general revenue bond issue.

Gorby, who lives in Balmoral, asked if the public would be given additional opportunities to speak out on the issue. Mayor Newman said: "I imagine several times."

Newman said that written comments received by the Stormwater Management Citizens Advisory Committee prior to its next meeting in about 30 days would be considered along with opinions recorded at Tuesday night's meeting.

Gorby was also quoted as saying: "A project like this is for the future of the community."

After noting that his Henderson utility cost is "the cheapest ... I've ever run across," he said: "I would gladly pay 79 cents to get Fourth Street fixed."

Gorby was referring to the monthly additional charge engineers estimate the city's 10,000 water-sewer customers would have to pay to finance a project that would eliminate the persistent flooding problem at Fourth and Green streets.

Fuller explained his company's assessment of stormwater management needs in 11 "problem areas" of the city. He said that a formal report in which priority areas will be recommended will be issued "in late February."

The city included estimated costs of providing a drainage network in the problem areas and of diverting the water to either Canoe Creek or the Ohio River.

Mayor Newman said that the engineers' report will be turned over to the citizens committee so that the committee can formulate recommendations to the city commission. Newman said that the study was undertaken after floodwaters severely damaged several local industries.

Newman said that damage figures from flooding of the past two years have not been compiled. He was quoted: "Kusan and Gamco suffered a lot of damage" last year, and Artfaire sustained "a half million dollar loss in a single flood."

He was further quoted:

"I don't know what the committee will recommend. They could say that maybe it's not worth the investment." But "before any action would be taken I think we would have another public hearing on financing."

Three commissioners—Allen Kenney, Bill Brown and Claud Hays—were quoted.

Kenney said that he believed most of his constituents "would like to have the problem studied and, if possible, fixed. I doubt if we could do it all at once, but maybe we could do it piecemeal [and] ... avoid large charges for anyone."

Brown said that he would prefer to wait for completion of the U.S. Corps of Engineers project to channelize the North Fork of Canoe Creek. "I think they said 85 percent of the flooding on Canoe Creek would be eliminated. We ought to try to do something about the problem." Brown added that the city might be able to fund a project from its general fund. "It might not cost the taxpayer nearly as much" as the Proctor-Davis-Ray plan, he said.

Hays said that the stormwater problem has existed for many years, but he said that current city officials "instead of throwing up our hands started a study to see what was needed and how much it would cost. We're not trying to force a $10 or $30 charge down anybody's throat."

Additional questions and comments came from others in the audience.

Don Crabtree, for example, noted that at current erosion rates a proposed 128-acre lake would be filled with silt in "slightly more than eight years." Fuller said that problem would fall under maintenance, which would be addressed in the design phase of the project.

Don Williams asked if the plan was designed to prevent primarily damage or inconvenience, and questioned whether insurance might provide a less expensive alternative. Fuller said that insurance is not available for buildings in a flood plain.

Charles Rettig wanted to know if only the residents included in the project area would be required to pay for the improvements. Fuller said that how the cost would be calculated could be determined on several bases. But he said that generally "it is felt that … everybody benefits, so everybody pays."

Eugene Gilbert criticized annexation of areas that require installation of costly city utilities. "If they build houses in the low areas, they should know they're going to have water problems," he said. "People in the affected areas should have to pay—not the taxpayers."

20

Police and Fire

Review Questions

1 List sources for police news.

2 Discuss *Topeka* (Kan.) *Capital-Journal* reporter Roger Aeschliman's philosophy of working with sources.

3 Why should police and fire reporters who normally cover hard news occasionally write feature stories about the people or the institutions they cover regularly?

4 The *Topeka* (Kan.) *Capital-Journal* never publishes the names of rape victims and their families. Do you agree with this policy? Why or why not?

5 The chapter emphasizes the importance of reporters' doing follow-up interviews with arresting officers and other officials when writing stories based on police reports. Why are these follow-ups important?

6 List information that should be included in most fire stories.

7 Under the subhead "Using Vivid Details: A Question of Taste," Roger Aeschliman provides his reasoning for having included a particularly gruesome quotation in a major fire story. Do you agree with his decision? Why or why not?

8 List information that should be included in most arrest stories.

9 List eight of the suggestions for beat reporters discussed in the chapter.

Suggested Exercises

1 What is the problem with the following lead paragraph?

> John Jones was arrested and booked into Adams County Jail for sexually assaulting a 17-year-old girl at the corner of Central and Commercial.

2 Information from a Tempe (Ariz.) Police Department activity log follows. Only the names and addresses have been changed. Write a story based on all the information available.

Incident: Aggravated assault/knife

Location: 100 E. Norwood, Tempe

Date: Monday

Time: 2340

Victim(s): Jeffrey Gordon Smith, 18, 210 E. Norwood, Tempe; William Russell Jones, 17, 137 E. Norwood, Tempe

Arrest made: No

Suspect(s): Unknown, 15 years old, white male, 5'8", 130 pounds, short, curly hair. Wearing jeans, Levis jacket. Carrying a knife with a 4-5" blade.

Details: Jones and Smith were searching the neighborhood around a friend's house for any suspects involved in a burglary from a vehicle at 210 E. Norwood. Jones and Smith located the described subject walking near 100 E. Norwood. They demanded that this subject tell them who he was, and what he was doing, when the subject pulled out a knife and told them not to "screw with" him. The suspect then chased Jones and Smith back to their vehicle with the knife held over his head. When Jones and Smith entered the vehicle, the suspect began trying to slash at Smith through the open passenger side window. The victims were able to drive away and there were no injuries.

Investigating officers: Cable/Cook

Supervisor: Forbes

Additional information from a Tempe Police Department incident report, written by an investigating officer, follows.

At approximately 2324 hours I was dispatched to 210 E. Norwood in regards to a burglary from a vehicle report. Upon my arrival at 2328 hours I contacted Mr. Michael J. Johnson, the complainant. Mr. Johnson advised the following: at approximately 2320 hours he heard a noise where his car was located and he went out to investigate.

Upon discovering his car had been burglarized, Mr. Johnson went back into the house to get his friend, Mr. Jeffrey G. Smith of 210 E. Norwood.

Smith and Johnson then searched the immediate area for suspects. None was found. At this time, approximately 2330 hours, a friend of theirs, Mr. William R. Jones of 137 E. Norwood, drove into Smith's driveway. Smith asked Jones to shine his lights on the area in front of the house and the area where the burglary took place (in the driveway just west of the house). He did and nothing was found. Smith then entered Jones' car, a 1979 Datsun, two-door, and they drove on Norwood hoping to find a suspect. Upon reaching Santa Cruz Drive, they headed north and then went west at the alley. They found nothing.

Upon approaching Grandview, they noticed an unknown, white male, 5'8" and 130 pounds, approximately 15 years of age, wearing blue jean jacket (fairly new), Levis (blue) and who had brown curly hair, standing by the corner of Grandview and Norwood. Upon approaching the suspect, they stopped the car (on Norwood) and Mr. Smith got out to ask him (suspect) some questions.

Smith explained to the suspect that a friend of theirs had just been "ripped off," and did he know anything about it. Then Jones asked the suspect where he was, and what was he doing about five minutes ago. The suspect stated he was at the store getting cigarettes and when Mr. Jones asked to see proof, the suspect became violent. He asked Smith if he wanted to "screw with him and screw with his brother." (The suspect then pointed to a residential dwelling, 110 E. Norwood, indicating that's where his brother lives.) The suspect then took out a knife, approximately 5" in length. The suspect then held the knife (opened) over his head and again asked Mr. Smith if he wanted to "screw with him."

Mr. Smith then went to get into the car and again the suspect repeated the threat by waving the knife toward Mr. Smith.

When Mr. Smith got into the car, the

suspect moved to the passenger window and began striking the door with the "butt end" of the knife. The suspect then reached through the open passenger window and made a stabbing gesture toward Mr. Smith.

As Mr. Jones was driving away, east on Norwood, the suspect was running alongside the vehicle still trying to stab Mr. Smith through the window. He was unable to keep up with the vehicle.

Mr. Jones then drove back toward 210 E. Norwood, parking his car one block east so the suspect would not know where Mr. Smith lives.

Upon completion of the burglary investigation, I went to 110 E. Norwood, the address that the suspect pointed to. I checked to see if lights were on in the house, they were, so I knocked on the door.

The door was answered by Mr. Gary E. Henderson, white male, 5'8", 135 pounds, brown hair, brown eyes, 21 years old, a resident of the house. I advised Mr. Henderson of the situation and he agreed to a one-on-one. The result was negative. Mr. Henderson said he would ask his roommates, who were home, if they had brothers fitting the description of the suspect. Neighbors in the area were not contacted due to the hour.

I then took three latent fingerprint cards from the passenger's door.

Mr. Smith is unsure as to whether he will aid in prosecution or not. Mr. Jones will aid in prosecution.

It should be noted that Mr. Smith and Jones felt threatened by the knife-swinging actions of the suspect. Neither victim sustained any injuries.

3 Information from a Tempe Police Department activity log follows. Only the names and some addresses have been changed. Write a story based on all the information available.

Incident: Burglary—nonresidence

Location: 106 E. University

Date: Monday

Time: 0315

Amount of loss/recovery: $741.10/$741.10

Arrest made: Yes

Suspect(s): John Q. Smyth

Age: 20

Address: 1501 S. Elm, Tempe

Details: Suspect was observed in the 1100 block of S. Ash Ave. looking into cars which were parked along the street. A mobile surveillance was established both in cars and on foot. The suspect was lost from view in the area of Myrtle/University. A perimeter was established in that area, and a few minutes later the suspect was observed walking southbound across University at Myrtle. The suspect was followed from that location to 10th/Maple while a marked patrol unit was responding to make contact. Prior to the arrival of the marked unit, the suspect was observed to be dropping something every few steps. On contact with the suspect, it was found that his pockets were stuffed with both paper money in various denominations plus several rolls of coins and loose change. The suspect was asked where he got the money, and he stated that he collects it. Officer Howard DeMasi began a search of the area where the suspect was last seen at Myrtle/University and found an unlocked bathroom door at the rear of Panhandler's Pizza, 106 E. University. DeMasi looked inside the bathroom and found that an inside wall that led to the interior of the business had been kicked in and entry had been made. The suspect was arrested and on his person was a key that unlocked the bathroom door that DeMasi had found unlocked. The suspect stated that he is a former employee of Panhandler's Pizza. An excellent job by Officer Ray Russell who first saw the suspect and established the surveillance. It was also discovered that the items he had been dropping on the ground were various denominations of money falling out of his pockets. A search of the route he followed from University/Myrtle was conducted and the money lost was recovered.

Additional information: Smyth was charged with third-degree burglary and felony theft and transferred to Maricopa County Jail in lieu of $6,850 bond.

4 Write a news story based on the following information, which is from an article in the *Colorado Springs* (Colo.) *Gazette Telegraph.*

There was a fire Tuesday at the rural Peyton home of Hugh Bennett and his wife, Josie. The Bennetts, who placed their ages at "80—thereabouts," watched Falcon and Peyton firefighters from the warmth of their vehicle at their ranch.

The couple began building the house in 1936. It was damaged by smoke and fire after a smoldering roof fire ignited. The Bennetts and an employee, Lily Curns, were not injured after smoke filled the home about 2 p.m.

Falcon Fire Chief Vern Kauffman said the chimney had a hole in it and started a fire that "we feel was smoldering up there since last night" in a space between the ceiling and roof. The chief said the Bennetts had smelled smoke off and on during the day.

Firefighters estimated the damage at $15,000.

Bennett was quoted: "It's pretty bad. We're grateful to the Falcon Fire Department—they were here just that quick."

The Fire Department was called at about 2 p.m. At 2:40 the fire was reported under control. Falcon volunteers responded to the scene first, then requested aid from Peyton volunteers about 15 minutes later. Before the fire was under control, 20 firefighters were there.

Kauffman said "there was just smoke" when the first units arrived. He continued: "There was some flame, but not much. It basically stayed between the two roofs in a smoldering phase until we opened it up."

The Bennetts had been ranching the property for 45 years. After starting to build the house in 1936, they added to it, according to Bennett, "as we could afford it."

The Bennetts kept their good humor as firefighters and newspeople tramped across their property. The property was marked at the entrance by a wood painting of Pikes Peak.

The Bennetts had to leave the house quickly when it filled with smoke. The Bennetts were not able to take much with them. Still, Bennett said his wife "just had to go get this, that and the other."

Mrs. Bennett lifted a foot to show reporters she still was wearing slippers. It was one of the few items she removed from the house.

Bennett was quoted: "We travel light."

Both Mr. and Mrs. Bennett had been sick this past month. Tuesday was the first time Mrs. Bennett had been outside in three weeks, she said.

Bennett said his two hired hands, who live in other houses on the property, immediately ran to the house to help. "We got out under our own power, but you're never sure," Bennett said.

5 Write a news story based on the following information, which is from an article published on a Monday in the *Fairbanks* (Alaska) *Daily News-Miner.*

There were three separate fires over the weekend in the Fairbanks area. It was February, and there were arctic temperatures.

A fire at the Klondike Inn occurred Friday afternoon. It caused damage estimated between $25,000 and $30,000. No injuries were reported. The cause of the fire is under investigation. City fire inspector Eric Mohrmann is investigating. Mohrmann said that fire damage was confined to Room 246. It had been vacant for some time. The smoke and water damage spread to adjoining units of the hotel at 1316 Rewak.

M/J Rentals on the Richardson Highway was damaged by a fire early Sunday morning. Damage was estimated at $70,000. Chief Charles Lundfelt of the North Star Volunteer Fire Department said that a passerby spotted the blaze and reported it at 5:22 a.m. Sunday to Alaska State Troopers. Lundfelt said that the fire began in the business's furnace room. The fire is under investigation by the state fire marshal's office. The chief said that the building is worth $350,000. Its contents are worth $1.5 million. The contents were not damaged. Called to the fire were four engines and 19 firefighters from the North Star department. Firefighters worked in 34-below temperatures.

Damage estimated at $7,600 was sustained at the Great Land Hotel, 723 First Ave. The hotel was evacuated Sunday afternoon after a fire in a maintenance room spread smoke throughout the building. The cause of the fire was attributed to spontaneous combustion of rags used for staining. No one was injured. The hotel was filled with smoke when city firefighters arrived. First, the firefighters searched upper floors for the blaze. They could not find it. It was eventually traced to the maintenance office in the basement. The hotel sprinkler system controlled the fire until firefighters extinguished it. The city fire report said that smoke apparently spread through the building because some stairway doors were propped open. Smoke was cleared from the building after all the stairway doors and doors to the roof were opened. Guests staying at the hotel stood outside in sub-zero temperatures as firefighters brought in fans to clear the hallways of smoke. Mohrmann said that drying oils, when exposed to the atmosphere, are subject to spontaneous combustion. Cause of the fire was traced to rags that had been used a couple of hours earlier for staining wood trim. The rags were placed in a plastic garbage can, not in a sealed metal bucket. The rags began to smolder and eventually caught fire. They melted the can they were in. University of Alaska Fire Department also responded to the fire. This is part of the city's mutual aid plan.

6 Write a news story based on the information on the following pages, which is from an Arizona Traffic Accident Report Form.

ARIZONA TRAFFIC ACCIDENT REPORT

FORWARD COPY TO ARIZONA DEPARTMENT OF TRANSPORTATION ACCIDENT RECORDS ANALYSIS UNIT 222E 206 S. 17th AVE., PHOENIX, ARIZONA 85007

1

REPORT ID	DATE YEAR	MONTH	DAY	HOUR	AGENCY USE	AGENCY REPORT NUMBER
	87	03	17	1703		87-29105

NCIC NO	OFFICER'S ID NO.	DAY OF WK
0717	03236	3

INJURY SEVERITY CLASSIFICATION: 1 NO INJURY; 2 POSSIBLE INJURY; 3 NON-INCAPACITATING EVIDENT; 4 INCAPACITATING; 5 FATAL; 6 UNKNOWN

TOTAL NO. OF SHEETS ____

2 TOTAL UNITS: 3 | TOTAL INJURIES: 1 | TOTAL FATALITIES: 1 | ESTIMATED TOTAL DAMAGE: ■ OVER MINIMUM ☐ UNDER MINIMUM | ■ FATAL ☐ HIT/RUN ☐ GOVT. PROP. | DISTRICT OR GRID NO.: BC02

3 LOCATION

NAME OF STREET OR HIGHWAY ON: S, Extension Rd. | ■ INSIDE ☐ OUTSIDE | CITY: mesa | COUNTY: maricopa

INTERSECTING STREET, ROAD/M.P. OR R.P.: ☐ AT ■ FROM Emerald Ave | ■ NORTH ☐ SOUTH ☐ EAST ☐ WEST | ☐ PLUS ☐ MINUS | DISTANCE: 32 | ☐ MILES ■ FEET

4 TRAFFIC UNIT NO.

STATE	CLASS	LICENSE OR SOCIAL SECURITY NUMBER	■ DRIVER ☐ PEDESTRIAN ☐ PEDALCYCLIST	NAME	SEX	INJ
AZ	2	M43571		John Goff	M	1

RESTRICTIONS	DATE OF BIRTH	ADDRESS	CITY	STATE
None	1-12-53	1920 W. Lindner #2	Mesa	AZ

PLATE NUMBER	STATE	YEAR	■ SAME AS DRIVER	OWNER'S NAME	ADDRESS	CITY	STATE
5515-NV	AZ	87					

COLOR	YEAR	MAKE	BODY STYLE	☐ CAMPER	VIN	RESTRAINT USED
TAN	82	Chevy	Pickup		1GCE4H322346	☐ YES ■ NO ☐ UNK

REMOVED TO	REMOVED BY	ORDERS OF	POSTED SPEED LIMIT	OFC EST SPEED	OFC EST REAS
Service	Driver	Driver	35	35	35

TRAILER (OTHER UNIT) PLATE NO | STATE | YEAR | DESCRIPTION OF TRAILER OR OTHER UNIT | DR'S EST SPEED: 35

TRAFFIC UNIT NO.

STATE	CLASS	LICENSE OR SOCIAL SECURITY NO.	☐ DRIVER ■ PEDESTRIAN ☐ PEDALCYCLIST	NAME	SEX	INJ
				Melissa J. Green	F	5

RESTRICTIONS	DATE OF BIRTH	ADDRESS	CITY	STATE
	4-5-72	144 E Grove St.	Mesa	AZ

PLATE NUMBER | STATE | YEAR | ☐ SAME AS DRIVER | OWNER'S NAME | ADDRESS | CITY | STATE

COLOR | YEAR | MAKE | BODY STYLE | ☐ CAMPER | VIN | RESTRAINT USED ☐ YES ☐ NO ☐ UNK

REMOVED TO | REMOVED BY | ORDERS OF | POSTED SPEED LIMIT | OFC EST SPEED | OFC EST REAS

TRAILER (OTHER UNIT) PLATE NO. | STATE | YEAR | DESCRIPTION OF TRAILER OR OTHER UNIT | DR'S EST SPEED

5 PASSENGERS

SEATING POSITION DIAGRAM: 07 04 01 / 08 05 02 ▶ / 09 06 03; 10 NOT IN PASSENGER COMPART; 11 MOTORCYCLE, BUS; 12 OTHER; 13 UNKNOWN; 14 PEDALCYCLE

RU - RESTRAINT USED: Y-YES N-NO UK-UNK | HU - HELMET USAGE: Y-YES N-NO UK-UNK

INJURED TAKEN TO/BY: Phx. St. Joseph's Hosp. - Air-evac. Dead on arrival

UNIT	SEAT POS	RU	NAME	ADDRESS	CITY	STATE	HU	AGE	SEX	INJ
			None							

6 OTHER PROPERTY DAMAGE (DESCRIBE): None

OWNER'S NAME | ADDRESS | CITY | STATE | TELEPHONE NUMBER

7 WITNESSES

NAME	ADDRESS	CITY	STATE	TELEPHONE NUMBER	AGE
Michael Platzer	94 N. Pasadena St.	Mesa	AZ	None	20
Vinnie Sabre	117 W. Mesquite	Chandler	AZ	None	16

8 ARRESTS

NAME	A.R.S. NO. OR CITY CODE	CITATION/ARREST NUMBER(S)
John Goff	28-792A	Failure to yield to ped in x-walk; 136470

9 PHOTOS TAKEN: ■ YES ☐ NO | PHOTOGRAPHER'S NAME, ID NUMBER, AND AGENCY | INVEST AT SCENE ■ YES ☐ NO | DATE INVEST: 3-17-87 | TIME INVEST: 1728

OFFICER'S SIGNATURE AND ID NUMBER: Officer John Szczepanski #3236 | AGENCY: Mesa Police | DATE COMPLETED: 4-8-87

87-29105

10 - DIAGRAM

see supplement

11 - INDICATE NORTH

12 - SKIDDING OCCURED

[x] YES [ ] NO

INDICATE WHICH VEHICLES SKIDDED BY NUMBER: 1

13 - ACCIDENT MEASUREMENTS

see supplement

14 - DESCRIBE WHAT HAPPENED

Unit #1 was southbound on S. Extension when it hit units #2 & 3 who were crossing Extension from East to west at Emerald

15 - CLASSIFICATION BY TYPE

YES NO
[ ] [x] RAN OFF ROADWAY PRIOR TO FIRST HARMFUL EVENT

COLLISION BETWEEN A MOTOR VEHICLE IN TRANSPORT AND
1 [x] PEDESTRIAN
2 [ ] MOTOR VEHICLE
3 [ ] RAILWAY TRAIN
4 [ ] PEDALCYCLIST
5 [ ] ANIMAL
6 [ ] FIXED OBJECT
7 [ ] OTHER OBJECT

NONCOLLISION INVOLVING A MOTOR VEHICLE IN TRANSPORT
8 [ ] OVERTURNING
9 [ ] OTHER NONCOLLISION

16 - LIGHT CONDITION

CHECK ONLY ONE
1 [x] DAYLIGHT
2 [ ] DAWN OR DUSK
3 [ ] DARKNESS

YES NO
1 [x] [ ] STREET LIGHT
2 [ ] [x] STREET LIGHT FUNCTIONING

17 - WEATHER CONDITIONS

CHECK ONLY ONE
1 [ ] CLEAR
2 [ ] RAINING
3 [x] CLOUDY
4 [ ] SNOWING
5 [ ] STRONG WIND
6 [ ] DUST
7 [ ] FOG

18 - ROAD SURFACE TYPE

CHECK ONLY ONE
1 [x] ASPHALT
2 [ ] CONCRETE
3 [ ] GRAVEL
4 [ ] DIRT
5 [ ] OTHER

19 - TYPE OF LOCATION

CHECK ONLY ONE
1 [ ] INTERSECTION
2 [x] JUNCTION AREA
3 [ ] NON-JUNCTION AREA
4 [ ] DRIVEWAY ACCESS
5 [ ] ALLEY ACCESS

20 - INTERSECTION RELATED

[ ] YES [ ] NO

21 - SPECIAL LOCATION

CHECK ONLY ONE
1 [ ] SCHOOL CROSSING
2 [x] PEDESTRIAN CROSSWALK (STRIPED)
3 [ ] PEDESTRIAN CROSSWALK (NO STRIPING)
4 [ ] BRIDGE
5 [ ] TUNNEL
6 [ ] RR CROSSING
7 [ ] ALLEY
8 [ ] BIKE PATH
9 [ ] 2-WAY LEFT TURN LANE

22 - UNUSUAL ROAD CONDITION

CHECK ONLY ONE
1 [ ] UNDER CONSTRUCTION, TRAFFIC ALLOWED
2 [ ] UNDER CONSTRUCTION, NO TRAFFIC ALLOWED
3 [ ] UNDER REPAIRS
4 [ ] HOLES, RUTS, BUMPS
5 [ ] OBSTRUCTION - PROTECTED
6 [ ] OBSTRUCTION - UNPROTECTED
7 [ ] OBSTRUCTION - UNLIGHTED AT NIGHT
8 [ ] DEFECTIVE SHOULDERS
9 [ ] CHANGING ROAD WIDTH
10 [ ] FLOODED
11 [ ] TEMPORARY LANE CLOSURE

23 - TRAFFIC CONTROL DEVICES

LEGEND A - DEVICE PRESENT
B - DAMAGED OR NON-FUNCTIONAL PRIOR TO ACCIDENT

CHECK ANY THAT APPLY
A B
1 [ ] [ ] STOP AND GO SIGNAL
2 [ ] [ ] YIELD SIGN
3 [ ] [ ] STOP SIGN
4 [ ] [ ] WARNING SIGN
5 [ ] [ ] RAILROAD SIGNAL
6 [ ] [ ] FLASHING SIGNAL
7 [ ] [ ] FLAGMAN OR OFFICER

24 - NON-INTERSECTION ROAD CHARACTER

CHECK ONLY ONE
1 [x] 2-WAY, STRIPED CENTERLINE
2 [ ] 2-WAY, NO STRIPE
3 [ ] 2-WAY, PAINTED MEDIAN
4 [ ] 2-WAY, RAISED MEDIAN
5 [ ] 2-WAY, BARRIER MEDIAN
6 [ ] 2-WAY, DEPRESSED MEDIAN
7 [ ] 2-WAY, EXTENDED MEDIAN
8 [ ] 1-WAY STREET

25 - ROAD GRADE

CHECK ONLY ONE
1 [x] LEVEL
2 [ ] DOWNGRADE
3 [ ] UPGRADE
4 [ ] HILLCREST
5 [ ] DIP

26 - UNUSUAL ROAD SURFACE CONDITION

CHECK ONLY ONE
1 [ ] WET
2 [ ] LOOSE SAND, DIRT OR GRAVEL
3 [ ] SNOWY, ICY
4 [ ] FRESH OIL
5 [ ] OTHER
6 [ ] UNKNOWN

27 - PHYSICAL CONDITION

TWO CHOICES PER PERSON MAY BE SELECTED
1 2
1 [x] [ ] NO APPARENT DEFECTS
2 [ ] [ ] HAD BEEN DRINKING
3 [ ] [ ] APPEARED TO BE UNDER INFLUENCE OF DRUGS
4 [ ] [ ] ILL - ABILITY INFLUENCED
5 [ ] [ ] SLEEPY - FATIGUED
6 [ ] [ ] OTHER BODILY DEFECTS, INFIRMITIES
7 [ ] [ ] UNKNOWN

28 - VIOLATIONS / BEHAVIOR

TWO CHOICES PER PERSON MAY BE SELECTED
1 2
1 [ ] [ ] NO IMPROPER DRIVING
2 [ ] [ ] SPEED TOO FAST FOR CONDITIONS
3 [ ] [ ] EXCEEDED LAWFUL SPEED
4 [x] [ ] FAILED TO YIELD RIGHT-OF-WAY
5 [ ] [ ] FOLLOWED TOO CLOSELY
6 [ ] [ ] RAN STOP SIGN
7 [ ] [ ] DISREGARDED TRAFFIC SIGNAL
8 [ ] [ ] MADE IMPROPER TURN
9 [ ] [ ] DROVE IN OPPOSING TRAFFIC LANE
10 [ ] [ ] KNOWINGLY OPERATED WITH FAULTY OR MISSING EQUIPMENT
11 [ ] [ ] REQUIRED MOTORCYCLE SAFETY EQUIPMENT NOT USED
12 [ ] [ ] PASSED IN NO PASSING ZONE
13 [ ] [ ] UNSAFE LANE CHANGE
14 [ ] [ ] OTHER UNSAFE PASSING
15 [x] [x] INATTENTION
16 [ ] [ ] DID NOT USE CROSSWALK
17 [ ] [ ] WALKED ON WRONG SIDE OF ROAD
18 [ ] [ ] OTHER
19 [ ] [ ] UNKNOWN

29 - VEHICLE CONDITION

TWO CHOICES PER VEHICLE MAY BE SELECTED
1 2
1 [x] [ ] NO APPARENT DEFECTS
2 [ ] [ ] DEFECTIVE BRAKES
3 [ ] [ ] DEFECTIVE STEERING
4 [ ] [ ] DEFECTIVE HEADLIGHTS
5 [ ] [ ] DEFECTIVE TAIL LIGHTS
6 [ ] [ ] DEFECTIVE TURN-SIGNAL
7 [ ] [ ] PUNCTURE OR BLOWOUT
8 [ ] [ ] ONE OR MORE SMOOTH TIRES
9 [ ] [ ] FIRE
10 [ ] [ ] DEFECTIVE WINDSHIELD WIPER
11 [ ] [ ] DEFECTIVE EXHAUST SYSTEM
12 [ ] [ ] OTHER DEFECTS
13 [ ] [ ] NO TRAILER BRAKES
14 [ ] [ ] UNKNOWN

30 - TRAFFIC UNIT ACTION

CHECK ONE PER UNIT
1 2
1 [x] [ ] GOING STRAIGHT AHEAD
2 [ ] [ ] SLOWING IN TRAFFICWAY
3 [ ] [ ] STOPPED IN TRAFFICWAY
4 [ ] [ ] MAKING LEFT TURN
5 [ ] [ ] MAKING RIGHT TURN
6 [ ] [ ] MAKING U TURN
7 [ ] [ ] ENTERING ALLEY OR DRIVEWAY
8 [ ] [ ] LEAVING ALLEY OR DRIVEWAY
9 [ ] [ ] OVERTAKING/PASSING
10 [ ] [ ] CHANGING LANES
11 [ ] [ ] BACKING
12 [ ] [ ] AVOIDING VEHICLE, OBJECT, PEDESTRIAN
13 [ ] [ ] ENTERING PARKING POSITION
14 [ ] [ ] LEAVING PARKING POSITION
15 [ ] [ ] PROPERLY PARKED
16 [ ] [ ] IMPROPERLY PARKED
17 [ ] [ ] DRIVERLESS MOVING VEHICLE
18 [ ] [x] CROSSING ROAD
19 [ ] [ ] WALKING WITH TRAFFIC
20 [ ] [ ] WALKING AGAINST TRAFFIC
21 [ ] [ ] STANDING
22 [ ] [ ] LYING
23 [ ] [ ] GETTING ON OR OFF VEHICLE
24 [ ] [ ] WORKING ON OR PUSHING VEHICLE
25 [ ] [ ] WORKING ON ROAD
26 [ ] [ ] OTHER
27 [ ] [ ] UNKNOWN

31 - VISION OBSCUREMENT

CHECK ONE PER UNIT
1 2
1 [x] [x] NOT OBSCURED
2 [ ] [ ] BY PARKED STOPPED VEHICLE
3 [ ] [ ] BY MOVING VEHICLE
4 [ ] [ ] BY BUILDING
5 [ ] [ ] BY EMBANKMENT
6 [ ] [ ] BY SIGNBOARD
7 [ ] [ ] BY HILLCREST
8 [ ] [ ] BY LOAD ON VEHICLE
9 [ ] [ ] BY TREES, BUSHES
10 [ ] [ ] BY HEADLIGHT
11 [ ] [ ] BY SUN GLARE
12 [ ] [ ] BECAUSE OF BAD WEATHER
13 [ ] [ ] OTHER
14 [ ] [ ] RAIN, SNOW, FOG ON WINDSHIELD
15 [ ] [ ] WINDSHIELD OBSCURED - OTHER
16 [ ] [ ] UNKNOWN

32 - MOTORCYCLE HELMET USED

CHECK ONE PER UNIT
1 2
[ ] [ ] YES
[ ] [ ] NO
[ ] [ ] UNKNOWN

01-2704 R1-84 BACK

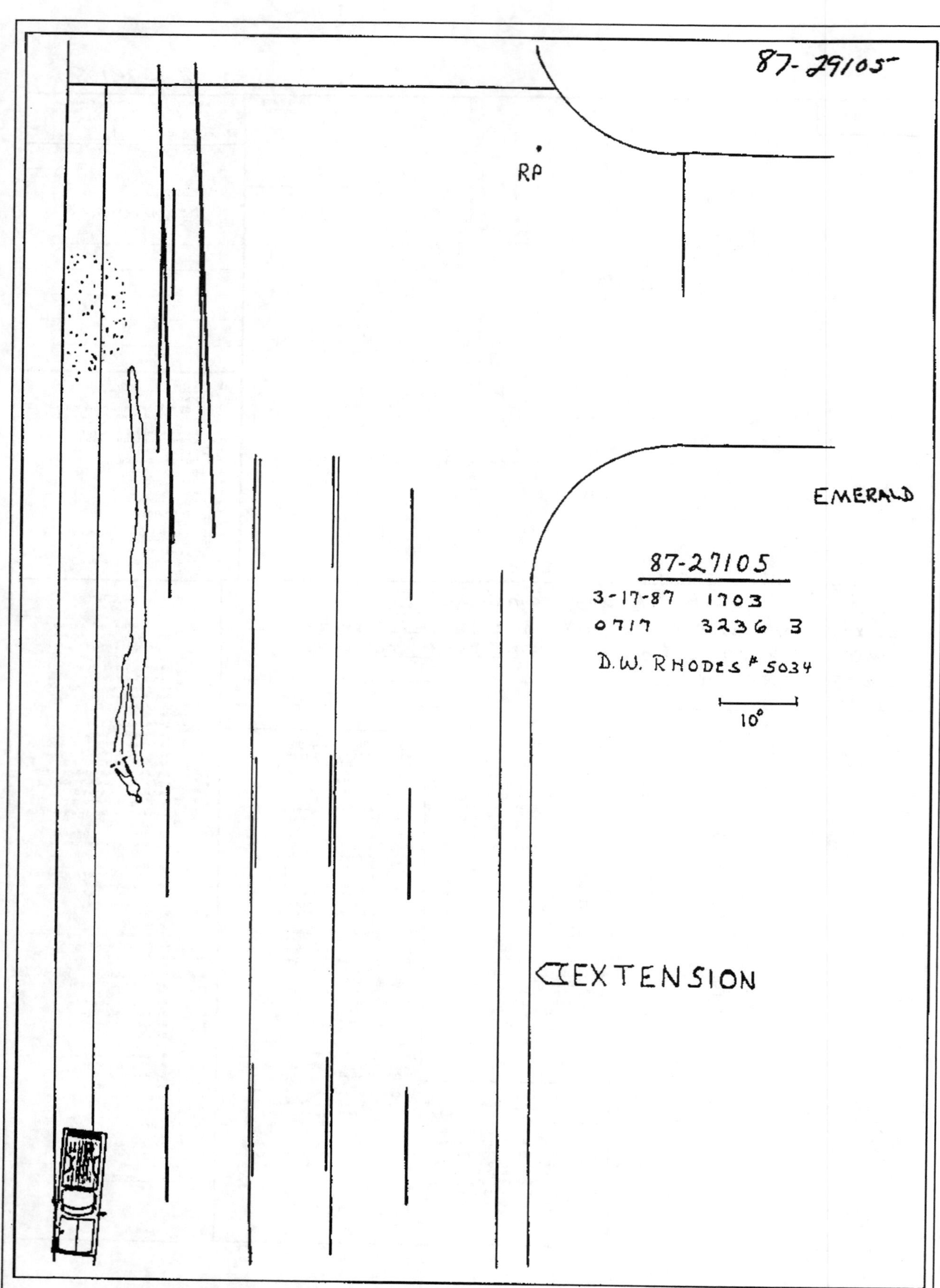
87-29105
RP
EMERALD
87-27105
3-17-87 1703
0717 3236 3
D.W. RHODES #5034
10'
EXTENSION

01-2706 R1/77 (BACK)

ACCIDENT DESCRIPTION
(Narrative)

On 3/17/87 at 1716 hrs I was on duty at the main police station and was telephoned by radio personnel and told of a serious injury accident in the 900 block of south Extension Road. I was told that the accident was a car-pedestrian and that a helicopter ambulance was being called to the accident scene. Upon my arrival I learned that the driver of a Chevy pickup was southbound on Extension and the victim, Melissa J. Green and a friend, Vinnie Sabre, were going to a baseball game at their school and were crossing Extension in the crosswalk at Emerald. They were crossing west to east and had crossed most of the roadway when a truck approached from the west side. Mr. Sabre told me he heard the screeching of tires and then seeing Miss Green going on top of the hood of the truck and then hitting the ground a distance away. He was not struck but said he felt the wind as the truck went by him. After talking to Mr. Sabre and other witnesses it appears as if the following happened: On 3/17/87 at 1703 hours Mr. John Goff was driving his tan Chevrolet pickup truck southbound on S. Extension, within the southbound curb lane. As he was approaching the intersection of Emerald, his attention was distracted by a baseball game which was being played at East High School on the west side of the street. At the same time, Vinnie Sabre and Melissa Green were crossing Extension from east to west within the crosswalk area. Sabre or Green did not realize that Goff's southbound pickup was approaching and was not stopping. Goff was not aware of the two pedestrians as they were right in front of the right front corner of his pickup. Sabre and Green had apparently realized that the pickup was coming and tried to get to the west curb and out of the way. The right front corner of Goff's truck contacted Green, and knocked her to the south where she skidded across the asphalt. Green came to rest within the southbound curb lane. Goff steered to the left and applied the brakes, causing the truck to skid across the asphalt.

INVESTIGATOR'S SIGNATURE: Officer John Szczepanski #3236 DATE: 4-8-87

01-2706 R1/77 (BACK)

ACCIDENT DESCRIPTION (Narrative)

87-29105 con't

On 3/31/87 I spoke with Mr. Palmer of the Maricopa County Attorney's Office, traffic unit. I explained the elements of the case to Mr. Palmer and he said he did not feel that elements existed to constitute criminal offenses. He referred the case to the Mesa City Magistrate Court.

On 4/8/87 I contacted Mr. Goff and at his Home I issued him citation #136470 for violation of Ariz. Revised Statues 28-792.A., failure to yield to a pedestrian in a crosswalk.

No further information.

INVESTIGATOR'S SIGNATURE Officer JOhn Szczepanski #3236 DATE 4/8/87

21

Courts

Review Questions

1 Discuss the three basic tiers in the federal court system.

2 Discuss the various courts in your state's judicial system.

3 Distinguish between criminal cases and civil cases.

4 Discuss plea bargaining.

5 Discuss the functions of a grand jury.

6 Discuss the potential newsworthy aspects of the following junctures in a criminal case.

a Arrest

b Lower-court arraignment

c Preliminary hearing

d Superior-court arraignment

e Jury selection

f Testimony

g Verdict

h Presentence hearing

i Sentencing

j Appeal

7 Discuss the importance of attributing information to court records.

8 Why should reporters try to be present when the jury returns with a verdict?

9 List primary human sources for reporters who cover litigation.

10 Define the following.

a Indictment

b Warrant

c Information

d Defendant

e True bill

f No bill

g Felony

h Misdemeanor

i Gag order

j Brief

k Docket

l Plaintiff

m Complaint

n Damages

o Deposition

p Settlement

Suggested Exercises

1 Assume that you are a reporter for a newspaper in your town. Using the information presented in exercises 1 to 5, write news stories at various junctures in a criminal case. First, use the following information to write an arrest story.

An 11-year-old girl, who had been missing for two days, was found dead last Saturday in a field four miles south of town. Her body was found by two teen-agers who were jogging on a country road. The name of the girl was Sally Jones. She was the daughter of Mr. and Mrs. Bill Jones.

The county coroner released a report Tuesday saying that the girl had been sexually assaulted and strangled and had been dead since the previous Thursday, June 20.

One week after the body was found, a 23-year-old man was arrested by police.

The man was identified by Police Chief Donald South as William J. Henderson. Henderson was arrested Saturday night in the county jail, where he had been for three days for a probation violation.

At a press conference Saturday evening, South said that he did not know whether Henderson had a criminal history of sex offenses. Henderson was employed as a construction worker by a local firm.

Henderson was being held for investigation of first-degree murder and sexual assault, according to South.

2 Write a story based on this description of the arraignment in Police Court.

Henderson was arraigned in Police Court on Monday. Through his attorney, public defender Paul Cummings, Henderson pleaded not guilty to charges of first-degree murder and sexual assault. The arraignment lasted 15 minutes. Henderson did not speak. The presiding judge was Fred Waters. The case was assigned to Police Court Judge Dean Gardner for an Aug. 5 preliminary hearing. Henderson was ordered held without bond in county jail.

3 Write a story about the preliminary hearing.

A preliminary hearing was held in Police Court on Thursday. The presiding judge was Dean Gardner. Gardner found that there was sufficient evidence for Henderson to be bound over for trial in Superior Court. Police Chief South testified that on the evening Miss Jones disappeared, Henderson had been seen a quarter mile from where her body was found. Gardner refused to set bond; he ordered that Henderson continue to be held in county jail.

4 Write a story about the arraignment in Superior Court.

Henderson was arraigned in Superior Court on Wednesday before Superior Court Judge David Glenn. Henderson pleaded not guilty to first-degree murder and sexual assault. He wore county jail garb. Trial was set for Nov. 10.

5 Write a story about the verdict.

Henderson was found guilty in Superior Court Thursday after a seven-day trial on charges of first-degree murder and sexual assault. The jury deliberated 35 minutes. Henderson showed no emotion as the verdict was read by Judge David Glenn. Jurors left the courtroom without comment.

A court official said that the six women jurors and two of the six men were crying as they left. The jury had spent most of the day listening to closing arguments by prosecuting attorney Terry Johnson and Paul Cummings, a public defender who represented Henderson. Cummings said that he would appeal. Glenn scheduled a presentence hearing for Nov. 28 and sentencing for Dec. 1.

6 Write a feature story based on the following information, which is from the *Plano* (Texas) *Star Courier.*

About 400 to 450 people are called to jury duty each week by the Collin County district clerk's office.

Sandra Simms is the county's jury clerk. She is responsible for mailing jury summonses. About one-third of those who are summoned choose to complain by telephone.

Simms has been jury clerk since 1985. She said that she thought she had heard just about every excuse. Still, every now and then a new one pops up.

The only people who are exempt from jury duty are those over 65, full-time students, those no longer living in the county, convicted felons and parents with children under the age of 10, but not those who work outside the home. In addition, some people have legitimate medical reasons for not serving.

Pay is not great. The county pays $7.50 a day for jury duty; average length of service is 2½ days, according to Simms.

Elected officials, lawyers, clergy, law enforcement officers and doctors are not exempt.

Most people call to complain or to get excused from jury duty. A lot mail in their protests. One of Simms' favorites is when a women mailed in an outline of a human body. It had arrows pointing to her various ailments. Simms said that the woman was still well enough to serve.

Occasionally, some people will come in person to voice their displeasure. Common complaints or excuses are that they are too busy, too important or too sensitive to sit in judgment of another person.

Some excuses are more bizarre. Simms cited a man who insisted that he should be excused because his dog was a diabetic. The man insisted that, because the dog required regular insulin injections, the master had to remain at home. The excuse did not work. The man served his jury duty, and the dog went to the veterinarian's office. Simms said that the man enjoyed his experience after all, but she did not know about the dog.

Another man said that he could not serve because he was an Elvis impersonator. The man always called from his car phone because he said that he was on the road entertaining all the time. Simms gave the man an extension—until he finished his tour.

Quotation from Simms: "Whenever he'd call he'd sound like he was at the bottom of a well. Maybe it was the connection, but he didn't sound anything like Elvis."

Simms said that she wished the man would have come to her office so that she could "see if he at least looks like Elvis."

Simms said that she is firm that all who are summoned must serve—at least eventually. She allows a month's extension for people who telephone in for almost any reason. However, for a second request, the person must come in person on the day he or she is scheduled for jury duty.

At this point, most people accept the responsibility, or at least resign themselves to the inevitability, Simms noted.

Simms said, however, that some people cannot be calmed. If this is the case, she refers them to District Clerk Hannah Kunkle.

Kunkle remembered one such "uncalmable person." He was a preacher who claimed that he should be exempt because he was booked years in advance going around the country saving souls.

Quotation from Kunkle: "I don't know what kind of evangelist he was. He was in my office, and I couldn't believe the swearing that came from his mouth."

It made no difference; the swearing preacher served.

Kunkle also mentioned an incident when a "doctor" called and said that his duty should be postponed again "because he said he had to see his patients." When Kunkle looked at the man's questionnaire, however, she found that the man was a veterinarian.

"He got no more postponements," she said.

Simms said that she empathizes with people who want to get out of jury duty because they are self-employed or because their employers won't pay their salaries while they serve. But, they still must serve.

7 Write a story based on the following information about a civil suit.

State Sen. John Blatchford filed suit in Nuckolls County Superior Court Friday in which the *Nelson Daily Tribune* was named the defendant.

It was a libel suit. Blatchford, in his complaint, said that the *Daily Tribune*'s article of May 15 that read in part, "State Sen. John Blatchford has carried his nephew Kevin Simpson on his payroll for the past two years at a salary of $28,500 annually even though the nephew reports for work only one day a week," was false, misleading and malicious.

In his complaint, Blatchford said that his nephew, a lawyer, is indeed on his payroll. But he is paid an annual consulting fee of $2,850.

Blatchford is asking for $200,000 compensatory damages and $1 million in punitive damages.

Blatchford told a news conference that "the *Daily Tribune* has been out to get me for years. Everyone knows that the *Daily Tribune* is a conservative Republican newspaper. Its publisher and editor have never appreciated my liberal stances on various issues."

Henry Moret, editor of the *Daily Tribune,* referred all questions to the newspaper's attorney. The attorney, however, could not be reached for comment.

Under existing American libel law, the state senator, as a public official, will have to prove that the newspaper acted with actual malice—knowing the story to be false or publishing it in reckless disregard for the truth. Public officials cannot collect libel damages merely by showing that the article was false.

8 Write a story based on the libel complaint filed by Ariel Sharon against Time Inc. You might also want to use this quotation by *Time* spokesman Brian Brown taken from an Associated Press story: "We're standing behind the story." Brown was also quoted as saying that the magazine had "every intention" of contesting the libel suit. The complaint is reprinted on the following pages.

UNITED STATES DISTRICT COURT
SOUTHERN DISTRICT OF NEW YORK

83CIV. 4660

JUDGE SOFAER

ARIEL SHARON, Plaintiff, -against- TIME INC., Defendant.	COMPLAINT Plaintiff Demands Trial By Jury

Plaintiff, ARIEL SHARON ("Sharon"), by his attorneys, Shea & Gould, as and for his Complaint against the defendant herein, alleges:

I

JURISDICTION

1. This Court has jurisdiction over this action pursuant to 28 U.S.C. §1332 and the principle of diversity jurisdiction since the parties are citizens of different states and the amount in controversy, exclusive of interest and costs, exceeds the sum of ten thousand dollars ($10,000).

2. Venue exists in this Court in that defendant Time Inc. has its principal place of business within the Southern District of New York.

II

THE PARTIES

3. Plaintiff Sharon is a citizen and resident of the State of Israel, a Minister of the government thereof and a member of its parliament known as the Knesset. Until the fourteenth day of February, 1983, plaintiff occupied the position of Minister of Defense.

4. Defendant Time Inc. is, upon information and belief, a corporation organized and existing under the laws of the State of New York with principal offices located at Rockefeller Center, New York, New York. Time Inc. is in the business of publishing, distributing and circulating a weekly news magazine known as Time which, upon information and belief, is published, circulated and sold throughout the United States, including the State and City of New York.

III

THE LIBEL

5. On or about September 28, 1982, the Government of Israel resolved to establish a commission of inquiry (the "Commission") to investigate certain events which occurred in or about September, 1982 in the Sabra and Shatila Palestinian neighborhoods in West Beirut, Lebanon. On or about February 9, 1983, the Commission issued a report of its investigation (the "Report"), which included a portion described as "Appendix B" which

-2-

the Commission determined to withhold from general publication for reasons of state security and foreign relations. (Such portion is hereinafter referred to as the "Secret Appendix.")

6. Upon information and belief, on or about February 21, 1983, defendant Time Inc. authored, composed and published an article captioned "The Verdict is Guilty" and subtitled "an Israeli commission apportions the blame for the Beirut massacre" (the "Article"), on pages 26 through 34 of the February 21, 1983 edition of Time. A copy of the Article as published is annexed hereto as Exhibit "A" and made a part hereof. The Article, which purported to describe and review the Commission's report, including the Secret Appendix thereto, contained the following false, defamatory and libelous matter of and concerning plaintiff Sharon personally and in his business and profession:

> " . . . one section of the report, known as Appendix "B", was not published at all, mainly for security reasons. That section contains the names of several intelligence agents referred to elsewhere in the report. TIME has learned that it also contains further details about Sharon's visit to the Gemayel family on the day after Bashir Gemayel's assassination. Sharon reportedly told the Gemayels that the Israeli army would be moving into West Beirut and that he expected the Christian forces to go into the Palestinian refugee camps. Sharon also reportedly discussed with the Gemayels the need for the Phalangists to take revenge for the assassination of Bashir, but the details of the conversation are not known . . ."

The above-quoted defamatory matter, hereinafter sometimes referred to as the "publication", is set forth on page 29 of the February 21, 1983 edition of Time.

7. The foregoing matter is false and defamatory in that it states that plaintiff discussed with the Gemayels the need for the Phalangists to take revenge against the West Beirut Palestinians and that plaintiff encouraged the Phalangists to perpetrate bloodshed among them. Plaintiff did not make any such statements nor did he participate in any such discussions as stated in the publication.

8. The foregoing matter is also false and defamatory in that, by purporting to describe the Secret Appendix as containing the statements and/or discussions allegedly made or engaged in by plaintiff, as set forth in the publication, to wit, that plaintiff discussed with the Gemayels the need for the Phalangists to take revenge for the assassination of Bashir Gemayel and that plaintiff encouraged the Phalangists to perpetrate bloodshed among the West Palestinians, the publication falsely attributes to the Commission a finding or determination that plaintiff in fact made such statements or participated in such discussions. Upon information and belief, the Secret Appendix does not contain any such finding or determination, nor does it describe or contain any such statements or discussions allegedly made or engaged in by plaintiff.

9. Upon information and belief, by the foregoing false and defamatory publication, defendant knowingly intended to and did depict plaintiff as having instigated and encouraged the Lebanese Phalangist forces to take revenge on the Palestinian population and to commit atrocities upon them.

10. Upon information and belief, the foregoing matter of and concerning plaintiff personally and in his business and profession and public office is false and, by reason of its contents, it is defamatory.

11. Upon information and belief, by virtue of the statements contained in the foregoing defamatory matter, defendant determined to, and did, author, compose and publish the foregoing matter in a manner maliciously intended to defame plaintiff and to subject him to public disgrace, scorn and ridicule, both personally and in his business and profession and public office.

12. Upon information and belief, at the time defendant authored, composed and published the defamatory matter, defendant knew that it was false, or failed to take the appropriate steps to ascertain whether the matter was true or false, and instead authored, composed and published it with reckless disregard as to its truth or falsity.

13. Upon information and belief, notwithstanding the existence of readily available means to confirm the presence of

the defamatory falsehoods contained in the publication, defendant, with malice aforethought and with knowledge that the foregoing defamatory and libelous matter was false or with reckless disregard as to its truth or falsity, determined to and did publish it.

14. By reason of the publication, plaintiff has been greatly injured personally, in his business and profession and in his public office, and will be further seriously injured in the future, has been held up to public contempt, disgrace, scorn, prejudice and ridicule, has suffered grave impairment of his good name, business and professional reputation and social standing, has lost the esteem and respect of his friends, acquaintances and business associates, and has suffered great pain and mental anguish, all to his damage in the sum of $25,000,000.

15. By reason of the foregoing, plaintiff is also entitled to punitive damages in the sum of $25,000,000.

WHEREFORE, plaintiff demands judgment against defendant in the amount of fifty million dollars ($50,000,000.00), together with the costs and disbursements of this action, and such other

-6-

and further relief as to the Court may seem just and proper.

Dated: New York, New York
June 22, 1983

SHEA & GOULD

By ______________________
A Member of the Firm
Attorneys for Plaintiff
330 Madison Avenue
New York, New York 10017
(212) 370-8000

PLEASE TAKE NOTICE that plaintiff demands a trial by jury.

Dated: New York, New York
June 22, 1983

SHEA & GOULD

By ______________________
A Member of the Firm
Attorneys for Plaintiff
330 Madison Avenue
New York, New York 10017
(212) 370-8000

9 Write a story about the outcome of Sharon's suit. Base your story on the following information, which is from an Associated Press story.

The federal jury ruled Thursday that *Time* magazine did not knowingly or recklessly publish a false story about Sharon.

Sharon lost his $50 million libel suit.

The jury had deliberated for 11 days. Previously, the jury had found that the *Time* article was false and that it was defamatory. But, because Sharon was a public figure, he had to show that the magazine had acted with actual malice—publishing the article knowing it to be false or in reckless disregard for the truth—in order to win the suit. In other words, the article must have been published with *Time* knowing it was false or seriously doubting its accuracy. The jury ruled that *Time* had not done so. The jury had been wrestling with the legal issue of actual malice since last Friday.

Jury foreman Richard Peter Zug read a statement that the jury had unanimously agreed upon. Zug's statement said that the jurors believed certain *Time* employees, especially Jerusalem correpondent David Halevy, had acted "negligently and even carelessly."

It should be remembered, however, that acting "negligently and carelessly" is not the same as acting in "reckless disregard."

Sharon and his wife were expressionless when the verdict was read. Later, on the courthouse steps, Sharon said: "I feel we have achieved what brought us here, and I accept it. It was a very long and hard struggle, and it was worth it.

"I came here to prove that *Time* magazine lied; we were able to prove that *Time* magazine did lie . . . and they were careless."

Also quoted was Sharon's lawyer, Milton Gould, who said that Sharon "didn't come here for any money. He came here for vindication, and he's been vindicated.... From a legal point of view ... we're very happy with the result."

Time managing editor Ray Cave was quoted: "Needless to say, we're immensely pleased with the verdict."

Also quoted was a written statement issued by the magazine: "*Time* feels strongly that the case should never have reached an American courtroom. It was brought by a foreign politician attempting to recoup his political fortunes."

Halevy was not present in the courtroom when Zug read his statement.

10 Excerpts from the official Supreme Court opinion in the case of *Miami Herald Publishing Co.* v. *Tornillo* are reprinted below. Write a news story for this afternoon's edition, based on your reading of the opinion. Assume that the opinion was handed down this morning.

MIAMI HERALD PUBLISHING CO. *v.* TORNILLO

Syllabus

MIAMI HERALD PUBLISHING CO., DIVISION OF KNIGHT NEWSPAPERS INC. *v.* TORNILLO

APPEAL FROM THE SUPREME COURT OF FLORIDA

No. 73-797. Argued April 17, 1974—Decided June 25, 1974

After appellant newspaper had refused to print appellee's replies to editorials critical of appellee's candidacy for state office, appellee brought suit in Florida Circuit Court seeking injunctive and declaratory relief and damages, based on Florida's "right to reply" statute that grants a political candidate a right of equal space to answer criticism and attacks on his record by a newspaper, and making it a misdemeanor for the newspaper to fail to comply. The Circuit Court held the statute unconstitutional as infringing on the freedom of the press and dismissed the action. The Florida Supreme Court reversed, holding that the statute did not violate constitutional guarantees, and that civil remedies, including damages, were available, and remanded to the trial court for further proceedings.

Held:

1. The Florida Supreme Court's judgment is "final" under 28 U.S.C.20§1257, and thus is ripe for review by this Court.

2. The statute violates the First Amendment's guarantee of a free press.

(a) Governmental compulsion on a newspaper to publish that which "reason" tells it should not be published is unconstitutional.

(b) The statute operates as a command by a State in the same sense as a statute or regulation forbidding appellant to publish specified matter.

(c) The statute exacts a penalty on the basis of the content of a newspaper by imposing additional printing, composing, and materials costs and by taking up space that could be devoted to other material the newspaper may have preferred to print.

(d) Even if a newspaper would face no additional costs to comply with the statute and would not be forced to forgo publication of news or opinion by the inclusion of a reply, the statute still fails to clear the First Amendment's barriers because of its intrusion into the function of editors in choosing what material goes into a newspaper and in deciding on the size and content of the paper and the treatment of public issues and officials.

Burger, C.J., delivered the opinion for a unanimous Court. Brennan, J., filed a concurring statement, in which Rehnquist, J., White, J., filed a concurring opinion.

Daniel P. S. Paul argued the cause for appellant. With him on the briefs were *James W. Beasley, Jr.,* and *Richard M. Schmidt, Jr.*

Jerome A. Barron argued the cause for appellee. With him on the brief were *Tobias Simon* and *Elizabeth duFresne.*

Opinion of the Court

Mr. Chief Justice Burger delivered the opinion of the Court.

The issue in this case is whether a state statute granting a political candidate a right to equal space to reply to criticism and attacks on his record by a newspaper violates the guarantees of a free press.

I

In the fall of 1972, appellee, Executive Director of the Classroom Teachers Association, apparently a teachers' collective-bargaining agent, was a candidate for the Florida House of Representatives. On September 20, 1972, and again on September 29, 1972, appellant printed editorials critical of appellee's candidacy.

[Footnote: The text of the September 20, 1972, editorial is as follows:

"The State's Laws and Pat Tornillo

"LOOK who's upholding the law!

"Pat Tornillo, boss of the Classroom Teachers Association and candidate for the State Legislature in the Oct. 3 runoff election, has denounced his opponent as lacking 'the knowledge to be a legislator, as evidenced by his failure to file a list of contributions to and expenditures of his campaign as required by law.'

"Czar Tornillo calls 'violation of this law inexcusable.'

"This is the same Pat Tornillo who led the CTA strike from February 19 to March 11, 1968, against the schoolchildren and taxpayers of Dade County. Call it whatever you will, it was an illegal act against the public interest and clearly prohibited by the statutes.

"We cannot say it would be illegal but certainly it would be inexcusable of the voters if they sent Pat Tornillo to Tallahassee to occupy the seat for District 103 in the House of Representatives."]

In response to these editorials appellee demanded that appellant print verbatim his replies, defending the role of the Classroom Teachers Association and the organization's accomplishments for the citizens of Dade County. Appellant declined to print the appellee's replies, and appellee brought suit in Circuit Court, Dade County, seeking declaratory and injunctive relief and actual and punitive damages in excess of $5,000. The action was premised on Florida statute §104.38 (1973), a "right of reply" statute which provides that if a candidate for nomination or election is assailed regarding his personal character or official record by a newspaper, the candidate has the right to demand that the newspaper print, free of cost to the candidate, any reply the candidate may make to the newspaper's charges. The reply must appear in as conspicuous a place and in the same kind of type as the charges which prompted the reply, provided it does not take up more space than the charges. Failure to comply with the statute constitutes a first-degree misdemeanor.

Appellant sought a declaration that §104.38 was unconstitutional. After an emergency hearing requested by appellee, the Circuit Court denied injunctive relief because, absent special circumstances, no injunction could properly issue against the commission of a crime, and held that §104.38 was unconstitutional as an infringement on the freedom of the press under the First and Fourteenth Amendments to the Constitution. The Circuit Court concluded that dictating what a newspaper must print was no different from dictating what it must not print. The Circuit Court Judge viewed the statute's vagueness as serving "to restrict and stifle protected expression." Appellee's cause was dismissed with prejudice.

On direct appeal, the Florida Supreme Court reversed, holding that §104.38 did not violate constitutional guarantees. It held that free speech was enhanced and not abridged by the Florida right-of-reply statute, which in that court's view, furthered the "broad societal interest in the free flow of information to the public." It also held that the statute is not impermissibly vague; the statute informs "those who are subject to it as to what conduct on their part will render them liable to its penalties." Civil remedies, including damages, were held to be available under this statute; the case was remanded to the trial court for further proceedings not inconsistent with the Florida Supreme Court's opinion.

We postponed consideration of the question of jurisdiction to the hearing of the case on the merits.

II

Although both parties contend that this Court has jurisdiction to review the judgment of the Florida Supreme Court, a suggestion was initially made that the judgment of the Florida Supreme Court might not be "final" under 28 U.S.C. §1257. In *North Dakota State Pharmacy Bd.* v. *Snyder's Stores,* 414 U.S. 156 (1973), we reviewed a judgment of the North Dakota Supreme Court, under which the case had been remanded so that further state proceedings could be conducted respecting Snyder's application for a permit to operate a drugstore. We held that to be a final judgment for purposes of our jurisdiction. Under the principles of finality enunciated in *Snyder's Stores,* the judgment of the Florida Supreme Court in this case is ripe for review by this court.

III

A

The challenged statute creates a right to reply to press criticism of a candidate for nomination or election. The statute was enacted in 1913, and this is only the second recorded case decided under its provisions.

Appellant contends the statute is void on its face because it purports to regulate the content of a newspaper in violation of the First Amendment. Alternatively it is urged that the statute is void for vagueness since no editor could know exactly what words would call the statute into operation. It is also contended that the statute fails to distinguish between critical comment which is and which is not defamatory.

B

The appellee and supporting advocates of an enforceable right of access to the press vigorously argue that government has an obligation to ensure that a wide variety of views reach the public. The contentions of access proponents will be set out in some detail. It is urged that at the time the First Amendment to the Constitution was ratified in 1791 as part of our Bill of Rights the press was broadly representative of the people it was serving. While many of the newspapers were intensely partisan and narrow in their views, the press collectively presented a broad range of opinions to readers.

Entry into publishing was inexpensive; pamphlets and books provided meaningful alternatives to the organized press for the expression of unpopular ideas and often treated events and expressed views not covered by conventional newspapers. A true marketplace of ideas existed in which there was relatively easy access to the channels of communication.

Access advocates submit that although newspapers of the present are superficially similar to those of 1791 the press of today is in reality very different from that known in the early years of our national existence. In the past half century a communications revolution has seen the introduction of radio and television into our lives, the promise of a global community through the use of communications satellites, and the specter of a "wired" nation by means of an expanding cable television network with two-way capabilities. The printed press, it is said, has not escaped the effects of this revolution. Newspapers have become big business and there are far fewer of them to serve a larger literate population. Chains of newspapers, national newspapers, national wire and news services, and one-newspaper towns, are the dominant features of a press that has become noncompetitive and enormously powerful and influential in its capacity to manipulate popular opinion and change the course of events. Major metropolitan newspapers have collaborated to establish news services national in scope. Such national organizations provide syndicated "interpretive reporting" as well as syndicated features and commentary, all of which can serve as part of the new school of "advocacy journalism."

The elimination of competing newspapers in most of our large cities, and the concentration of control of media that results from the only newspaper's being owned by the same interests which own a television station and a radio station, are important components of this trend toward concentration of control of outlets to inform the public.

The result of these vast changes has been to place in a few hands the power to inform the American people and shape public opinion. Much of the editorial opinion and commentary that is printed is that of syndicated columnists distributed nationwide and, as a result, we are told, on national and world issues there tends to be a homogeneity of editorial opinion, commentary, and interpretive analysis. The abuses of bias and manipulative reportage are, likewise, said to be the result of the vast accumulations of unreviewable power in the modern media empires. In effect, it is claimed, the public has lost any ability to respond or to contribute in a meaningful way to the debate on issues. The monopoly of the means of communication allows for little or no critical analysis of the media except in professional journals of very limited readership ....

We see that ... the Court has expressed sensitivity as to whether a restriction or requirement constituted the compulsion exerted by government on a newspaper to print that which it would not otherwise print. The clear implication has been that any such compulsion to publish that which "'reason' tells them should not be published" is unconstitutional. A responsible press is an undoubtedly desirable goal, but press responsibility is not mandated by the Constitution and like many other virtues it cannot be legislated.

Appellee's argument that the Florida statute does not amount to a restriction of appellant's right to speak because "the statute in question here has not prevented the *Miami Herald* from saying anything it wished" begs the core question. Compelling editors or publishers to publish that which "'reason' tells them should not be published" is what is at issue in this case. The Florida statute operates as a command in the same sense as a statute or regulation forbidding appellant to publish specified matter ....

Even if a newspaper would face no additional costs to comply with a compulsory access law and would not be forced to forgo publication of news or opinion by the inclusion of a reply, the Florida statute fails to clear the barriers of the First Amendment because of its intrusion into the function of editors. A newspaper is more than a passive receptacle or conduit for news, comment, and advertising. The choice of material to go into a newspaper, and the decisions made as to limitations on the size and content of the paper, and treatment of public issues and public officials—whether fair or unfair—constitute the exercise of editorial control and judgment. It has yet to be demonstrated how governmental regulation of this crucial process can be exercised consistent with First Amendment guarantees of a free press as they have evoloved to this time. Accordingly, the judgment of the Supreme Court of Florida is reversed.

It is so ordered.

11 Excerpts from the Supreme Court opinion in the case of *Texas* v. *Johnson* are reprinted below. Write a news story for this afternoon's edition, based on your reading of the opinion. Assume that the opinion was handed down this morning.

TEXAS, Petitioner *v.* Gregory Lee JOHNSON

No. 88-155. Argued March 21, 1989—Decided June 21, 1989

BRENNAN, J., delivered the opinion of the Court, in which MARSHALL, BLACKMUN, SCALIA, and KENNEDY, JJ., joined. KENNEDY, J., filed a concurring opinion. REHNQUIST, C.J., filed a dissenting opinion, in which WHITE and O'CONNOR, JJ., joined. STEVENS, J., filed a dissenting opinion.

Kathi Alyce Drew, Dallas, Tex., for petitioner.

William M. Kunstler, New York City, for respondent.

Justice BRENNAN delivered the opinion of the Court.

After publicly burning an American flag as a means of political protest, Gregory Lee Johnson was convicted of desecrating a flag in violation of Texas law. This case presents the question whether his conviction is consistent with the First Amendment. We hold that it is not.

I

While the Republican National Convention was taking place in Dallas in 1984, respondent Johnson participated in a political demonstration dubbed the "Republican War Chest Tour." As explained in literature distributed by the demonstrators and in speeches made by them, the purpose of this event was to protest the policies of the Reagan administration and of certain Dallas-based corporations. The demonstrators marched through the Dallas streets, chanting political slogans and stopping at several corporate locations to stage "die-ins" intended to dramatize the consequences of nuclear war. On several occasions they spray-painted the walls of buildings and overturned potted plants, but Johnson himself took no part in such activities. He did, however, accept an American flag handed to him by a fellow protester who had taken it from a flag pole outside one of the targeted buildings.

The demonstration ended in front of Dallas City Hall, where Johnson unfurled the American flag, doused it with kerosene, and set it on fire. While the flag burned, the protesters chanted, "America, the red, white, and blue, we spit on you." After the demonstrators dispersed, a witness to the flag-burning collected the flag's remains and buried them in his backyard. No one was physically injured or threatened with injury, though several witnesses testified that they had been seriously offended by the flag-burning.

Of the approximately 100 demonstrators, Johnson alone was charged with a crime. The only criminal offense with which he was charged was the desecration of a venerated object in violation of Tex. Penal Code Ann. §42.09(a)(3) (1989). After a trial, he was convicted, sentenced to one year in prison, and fined $2,000. The Court of Appeals for the Fifth District of Texas at Dallas affirmed Johnson's conviction, but the Texas Court of Criminal Appeals reversed, holding that the State could not, consistent with the First Amendment, punish Johnson for burning the flag in these circumstances.

The Court of Criminal Appeals began by recognizing that Johnson's conduct was symbolic speech protected by the First Amendment: "Given the context of an organized demonstration, speeches, slogans, and the distribution of literature, anyone who observed appellant's act would have understood the message that appellant intended to convey. The act for which appellant was convicted was clearly 'speech' contemplated by the First Amendment." To justify Johnson's conviction for engaging in symbolic speech, the State asserted two interests: preserving the flag as a symbol of national unity and preventing breaches of the peace. The Court of Criminal Appeals held that neither interest supported his conviction ....

As to the State's goal of preventing breaches of the peace, the court concluded that the flag-desecration statute was not drawn narrowly enough to encompass only those flag burnings that were likely to result in a serious disturbance of the peace. And in fact, the court emphasized, the flag burning in this particular case did not threaten such a reaction. "'Serious offense' occurred," the court admitted, "but there was no breach of peace nor does the record reflect that the situation was potentially explosive. One cannot equate 'serious offense' with incitement to breach the peace."

Because it reversed Johnson's conviction on the ground that §42.09 was unconstitutional as applied to him, the state court did not address Johnson's argument that the statute was, on its face, unconstitutionally vague and overbroad. We granted certiorari, and now affirm.

II

Johnson was convicted of flag desecration for burning the flag rather than for uttering insulting words. This fact somewhat complicates our consideration of his conviction under the First Amendment. We must first determine whether Johnson's burning of the flag constituted expressive conduct, permitting him to invoke the First Amendment in challenging his conviction ....

[1,2] The First Amendment literally forbids the abridgement only of "speech," but we have long recognized that its protection does not end at the spoken or written word. While we have rejected "the view that an apparently limitless variety of conduct can be labeled 'speech' whenever the person engaging in the conduct intends thereby to express an idea," *United States* v. *O'Brien,* we have acknowledged that conduct may be "sufficiently imbued with elements of communication to fall within the scope of the First and Fourteenth Amendments ...."

Especially pertinent to this case are our decisions recognizing the communicative nature of conduct relating to flags. Attaching a peace sign to the flag, *Spence,* saluting the flag, *Barnette,* and displaying a red flag, *Stromberg* v. *California,* we have held, all may find shelter under the First Amendment ....

The State of Texas conceded for purposes of its oral argument in this case that Johnson's conduct was expressive conduct, Tr. of Oral Arg. 4, and this concession seems to us as prudent as was Washington's in *Spence.* Johnson burned an American flag as part—indeed, as the culmination—of a political demonstration that coincided with the convening of the Republican Party and its renomination of Ronald Reagan for President. The expressive, overtly political nature of this conduct was both intentional and overwhelmingly apparent. At his trial, Johnson explained his reasons for burning the flag as follows: "The American Flag was burned as Ronald Reagan was being renominated as President. And a more powerful statement of symbolic speech, whether you agree with it or not, couldn't have been made at that time. It's quite a just position [juxtaposition]. We had new patriotism and no patriotism." In these circumstances, Johnson's burning of the flag was conduct "sufficiently imbued with elements of communication," *Spence,* to implicate the First Amendment.

III

[5] The Government generally has a freer hand in restricting expressive conduct than it has in restricting the written or

spoken word .... It is, in short, not simply the verbal or nonverbal nature of the expression, but the governmental interest at stake, that helps to determine whether a restriction on that expression is valid.

Thus, although we have recognized that where "'speech' and 'nonspeech' elements are combined in the same course of conduct, a sufficiently important governmental interest in regulating the nonspeech element can justify incidental limitations on First Amendment freedoms," *O'Brien.*

In order to decide whether *O'Brien's* test applied here, therefore, we must decide whether Texas has asserted an interest in support of Johnson's conviction that is unrelated to the suppression of expression. If we find that an interest asserted by the State is simply not implicated on the facts before us, we need not ask whether *O'Brien's* test applies. The State offers two separate interests to justify this conviction: preventing breaches of the peace, and preserving the flag as a symbol of nationhood and national unity. We hold that the first interest is not implicated on this record and that the second is related to the suppression of expression.

A

[6,7] Texas claims that its interest in preventing breaches of the peace justifies Johnson's conviction for flag desecration. However, no disturbance of the peace actually occurred or threatened to occur because of Johnson's burning of the flag. Although the State stresses the disruptive behavior of the protesters during their march toward City Hall, it admits that "no actual breach of the peace occurred at the time of the flagburning or in response to the flagburning." The State's emphasis on the protesters' disorderly actions prior to arriving at City Hall is not only somewhat surprising given that no charges were brought on the basis of this conduct, but it also fails to show that a disturbance of the peace was a likely reaction to *Johnson's* conduct. The only evidence offered by the State at Trial to show the reaction to Johnson's actions was the testimony of several persons who had been seriously offended by the flag-burning.

The State's position, therefore, amounts to a claim that an audience that takes serious offense at particular expression is necessarily likely to disturb the peace and that the expression may be prohibited on this basis. Our precedents do not countenance such a presumption. On the contrary, they recognize that a principal "function of free speech under our system of government is to invite dispute. It may indeed best serve its high purpose when it induces a condition of unrest, creates dissatisfaction with conditions as they are, or even stirs people to anger ...." It would be odd indeed to conclude *both* that "if it is the speaker's opinion that gives offense, that consequence is a reason for according it constitutional protection."

We thus conclude that the State's interest in maintaining order is not implicated on these facts. The State need not worry that our holding will disable it from preserving the peace. We do not suggest that the First Amendment forbids a State to prevent "imminent lawless action." And, in fact, Texas already has a statute specifically prohibiting breaches of the peace, Tex. Penal Code Ann. §42.01 (1989), which tends to confirm that Texas need not punish this flag desecration in order to keep the peace.

B

The State also asserts an interest in preserving the flag as a symbol of nationhood and national unity. In *Spence,* we acknowledged that the Government's interest in preserving the flag's special symbolic value "is directly related to expression in the context of activity" such as affixing a peace symbol to a flag. We are equally persuaded that this interest is related to expression in the case of Johnson's burning of the flag. The State, apparently, is concerned that such conduct will lead people to believe either that the flag does not stand for nationhood and national unity, but instead reflects other, less positive concepts, or that the concepts reflected in the flag do not in fact exist, that is, we do not enjoy unity as a Nation. These concerns blossom only when a person's treatment of the flag communicates some message, and thus are related "to the suppression of free expression" within the meaning of *O'Brien.* We are thus outside of *O'Brien's* test altogether.

IV

[8] It remains to consider whether the State's interest in preserving the flag as a symbol of nationhood and national unity justifies Johnson's conviction.

As in *Spence,* "[w]e are confronted with a case of prosecution for the expression of an idea through activity," and "[a]ccordingly, we must examine with particular care the interests advanced by [petitioner] to support its prosecution." Johnson was not, we add, prosecuted for the expression of just any idea; he was prosecuted for his expression of dissatisfaction with the policies of this country, expression situated at the core of our First Amendment values.

Moreover, Johnson was prosecuted because he knew that his politically charged expression would cause "serious offense." If he had burned the flag as a means of disposing of it because it was dirty or torn, he would not have been convicted of flag desecration under this Texas law: federal law designates burning as the preferred means of disposing of a flag "when it is in such condition that it is no longer a fitting emblem for display," and Texas has no quarrel with this means of disposal. The Texas law is thus not aimed at protecting the physical integrity of the flag in all circumstances, but is designed instead to protect it only against impairments that would cause serious offense to others. Texas concedes as much: "Section 42.09(b) reaches only those severe acts of physical abuse of the flag carried out in a way likely to be offensive. The statute mandates intentional or knowing abuse, that is, the kind of mistreatment that is not innocent, but rather is intentionally designed to seriously offend other individuals ...."

If there is a bedrock principle underlying the First Amendment, it is that the Government may not prohibit the expression of an idea simply because society finds the idea itself offensive or disagreeable.

We have not recognized an exception to this principle even where our flag has been involved. In *Street* v. *New York,* we held that a State may not criminally punish a person for uttering words critical of the flag. Rejecting the argument that the conviction could be sustained on the ground that Street had "failed to show the respect for our national symbol which may properly be demanded of every citizen," we concluded that "the constitutionally guaranteed 'freedom to be intellectually ... diverse or even contrary,' and the 'right to differ as to things that touch the heart of the existing order,' encompass the freedom to express publicly one's opinions which are defiant or contemptuous." Nor may the Government, we have held, compel conduct that would evince respect for the flag. "To sustain the compulsory flag salute we are required to say that a Bill of Rights which guards the individual's right to speak his own mind, left it open to public authorities to compel him to utter what is not in his mind ...."

It is not the State's ends, but its means, to which we object. It cannot be gainsaid that there is a special place reserved for the flag in this Nation, and thus we do not doubt that the Government has a legitimate interest in making efforts to "preserv[e] the national flag as an unalloyed symbol of our country ...."

The way to preserve the flag's special role is not to punish those who feel differently about these matters. It is to persuade them that they are wrong .... And, precisely because it is our flag that is involved, one's response to the flag-burner may exploit the uniquely persuasive power of the flag itself. We can imagine no more appropriate response to burning a flag than waving one's own, no better way to counter a flag-burner's message than by saluting the flag that burns, no surer means of preserving the dignity even of the flag that burned than by—as one witness here did—according its remains a respectful burial. We do not consecrate the flag by punishing its desecration, for in doing so we dilute the freedom that this cherished emblem represents.

V

Johnson was convicted for engaging in expressive conduct. The State's interest in preventing breaches of the peace does not support his conviction because Johnson's conduct did not threaten to disturb the peace. Nor does the State's interest in preserving the flag as a symbol of nationhood and national unity justify his criminal conviction for engaging in political expression. The judgment of the Texas Court of Criminal Appeals is therefore

Affirmed.

Justice KENNEDY, concurring.

I write not to qualify the words Justice BRENNAN chooses so well, for he says with power all that is necessary to explain our ruling. I join his opinion without reservation, but with keen sense that this case, like others before us from time to time, exacts its personal toll ....

Chief Justice REHNQUIST, with whom Justice WHITE and Justice O'CONNOR join, dissenting.

In holding this Texas statute unconstitutional, the Court ignores Justice Holmes' familiar aphorism that "a page of history is worth a volume of logic." For more than 200 years, the American flag has occupied a unique position as the symbol of our Nation, a uniqueness that justifies a governmental prohibition against flag burning in the way respondent Johnson did here.

At the time of the American Revolution, the flag served to unify the Thirteen Colonies at home, while obtaining recognition of national sovereignty abroad. Ralph Waldo Emerson's "Concord Hymn" describes the first skirmishes of the Revolutionary War in these lines:

"By the rude bridge that arched the flood
Their flag to April's breeze unfurled,
Here once the embattled farmers stood
And fired the shot heard round the world."

During that time, there were many colonial and regimental flags, adorned with such symbols as pine trees, beavers, anchors, and rattlesnakes, bearing slogans such as "Liberty or Death," "Hope," "An Appeal to Heaven," and "Don't Tread on Me." The first distinctive flag of the Colonies was the "Grand Union Flag"—with 13 stripes and a British flag in the left corner—which was flown for the first time on January 2, 1776, by troops of the Continental Army around Boston. By June 14, 1777, after we declared our independence from England, the Continental Congress resolved:

"That the flag of the thirteen United States be thirteen stripes, alternate red and white: that the union be thirteen stars, white in a blue field, representing a new constellation."

No other American symbol has been as universally honored as the flag. In 1931, Congress declared "The Star Spangled Banner" to be our national anthem. In 1949, Congress declared June 14th to be Flag Day. In 1987, John Philip Sousa's "The Stars and Stripes Forever" was designated as the national march. Congress has also established "The Pledge of Allegiance to the Flag" and the manner of its deliverance. The flag has appeared as the principal symbol on approximately 33 United States postal stamps and in the design of at least 43 more, more times than any other symbol.

The American flag, then, throughout more than 200 years of our history, has come to be the visible symbol embodying our Nation. It does not represent the views of any particular political party, and it does not represent any particular political philosophy. The flag is not simply another "idea" or "point of view" competing for recognition in the marketplace of ideas. Millions and millions of Americans regard it with an almost mystical reverence regardless of what sort of social, political, or philosophical beliefs they may have. I cannot agree that the First Amendment invalidates the Act of Congress, and the laws of 48 of the 50 States, which make criminal the public burning of the flag ....

The Court concludes its opinion with a regrettably patronizing civics lecture, presumably addressed to the Members of both

Houses of Congress, the members of the 48 states legislatures that enacted prohibitions against flag burning, and the troops fighting under that flag in Vietnam who objected to its being burned: "The way to preserve the flag's special role is not to punish those who feel differently about these matters. It is to persuade them that they are wrong." The Court's role as the final expositor of the Constitution is well established, but its role as a platonic guardian admonishing those responsible to public opinion as if they were truant school children has no similar place in our system of government. The cry of "no taxation without representation" animated those who revolted against the English Crown to found our Nation—the idea that those who submitted to government should have some say as to what kind of laws would be passed. Surely one of the high purposes of a democratic society is to legislate against conduct that is regarded as evil and profoundly offensive to the majority of people—whether it be murder, embezzlement, pollution, or flag burning.

Our Constitution wisely places limits on powers of legislative majorities to act, but the declaration of such limits by this Court "is, at all times, a question of much delicacy, which ought seldom, if ever, to be decided in the affirmative, in a doubtful case." Uncritical extension of constitutional protection to the burning of the flag risks the frustration of the very purpose for which organized governments are instituted. The Court decides that the American flag is just another symbol, about which not only must opinions pro and con be tolerated, but for which the most minimal public respect may not be enjoined. The government may conscript men into the Armed Forces where they must fight and perhaps die for the flag, but the government may not prohibit the public burning of the banner under which they fight. I would uphold the Texas statute as applied in this case.

Justice STEVENS, dissenting.

As the Court analyzes this case, it presents the question whether the State of Texas, or indeed the Federal Government, has the power to prohibit the public desecration of the American flag. The question is unique. In my judgment rules that apply to a host of other symbols, such as state flags, armbands, or various privately promoted emblems of political or commercial identity, are not necessarily controlling. Even if flag burning could be considered just another species of symbolic speech under the logical application of the rules that the Court has developed in its interpretation of the First Amendment in other contexts, this case has an intangible dimension that makes those rules inapplicable.

A country's flag is a symbol of more than "nationhood and national unity." It also signifies the ideas that characterize the society that has chosen that emblem as well as the special history that has animated the growth and power of those ideas. The fleurs-de-lis and the tricolor both symbolized "nationhood and national unity," but they had vastly different meanings. The message conveyed by some flags—the swastika, for example—may survive long after it has outlived its usefulness as a symbol of regimented unity in a particular nation.

So it is with the American flag. It is more than a proud symbol of the courage, the determination, and the gifts of nature that transformed 13 fledgling Colonies into a world power. It is a symbol of freedom, of equal opportunity, of religious tolerance, and of goodwill for other peoples who share our aspirations. The symbol carries its message to dissidents both at home and abroad who may have no interest at all in our national unity or survival ....

The Court is therefore quite wrong in blandly asserting that respondent "was prosecuted for his expression of dissatisfaction with the policies of this country, expression situated at the core of our First Amendment values ...."

The ideas of liberty and equality have been an irresistible force in motivating leaders like Patrick Henry, Susan B. Anthony, and Abraham Lincoln, schoolteachers like Nathan Hale and Booker T. Washington, the Philippine Scouts who fought at Bataan, and the soldiers who scaled the bluff at Omaha Beach. If those ideas are worth fighting for—and our history demonstrates that they are—it cannot be true that the flag that uniquely symbolizes their power is not itself worthy of protection from unnecessary desecration.

I respectfully dissent.

22

Sports

Review Questions

1 Summarize the evolution of sports writing styles in American newspapers during the 20th century.

2 Clichés and hyperbolic adjectives are found less frequently on today's sports pages. List other trends, and make additional observations about contemporary sports pages.

3 List some of the clichés you have encountered when reading sports stories.

4 Discuss how gathering statistics for high school contests can be different from gathering statistics for college contests.

5 Discuss procedures for gathering quotations from athletes and coaches after a contest.

6 Discuss different writing approaches for sports stories in A.M. newspapers and in P.M. newspapers.

7 List the essential details that should be contained in most game stories.

Suggested Exercises

1 Edit the following sentences to conform to AP style.

a The coach looked to the bull pen, then to centerfield, and then made the pitching change.

b Johnson's diving catch was a major league play.

c Monday will feature a twi-night doubleheader.

d The 6'5" forward led both teams in scoring.

e Bill's father was an All-American basketball player in college.

f Quarter back's generally get all the glory, but line men have to work awfully hard.

g Smith's bogie on the eighteenth hole cost him the golf championship.

h Crandall won the 100-meter dash in :10.35.

i Brown earned the reputation of being the best back courtman in the league.

j Bennett's lay-up won the game.

k Both schools hope to make the play offs.

2 Write a game story based on the following information, which is from an Associated Press story.

Dateline—Evanston, Ill.

Penn State's Joe Paterno tied Alabama's Bear Bryant on Saturday for most Division I football victories: 323. With a win at home against Ohio State next week, Paterno would become the all-time winningest coach.

Penn State entered the game against Northwestern averaging just eight points a contest; it also had the nation's worst rushing offense. But the Nittany Lions came out of their slumber on this Saturday afternoon. Penn State, 1–4 overall and 1–3 in the Big Ten, accumulated 501 yards of total offense against a porous Northwestern defense, including a season-high 213 rushing. Paterno's team had scored only 31 points in its previous four games.

The Nittany Lions came from behind five times during the afternoon, scoring the winning touchdown with 22 seconds left in the contest. The final score was 38–35. Northwestern, 4–2 overall and 2–2 in the Big Ten, had entered the game ranked No. 22.

Zack Mills, a redshirt freshman, was the hero. He came off the bench with 1:39 remaining and led Penn State to its winning score after junior Matt Senneca, the starting quarterback who was enjoying his best collegiate game ever, was knocked out on a jarring tackle.

The drive, with Senneca at the controls, had started at the Penn State 31 yard line. Mills entered the game with the ball on the Penn State 48, and his team was facing second-and-10.

Quotation—Paterno said: "This is the kind of game you love. I'm going to go home and get in trouble with a good stiff bourbon. Then I'm going to take a nap and get out some Ohio State tapes."

Paterno is 74 years old. His record stands at 323–94–3 in 36 seasons at Penn State. Bryant was 323–85–17 in 38 seasons at Maryland, Texas A&M and Alabama. Florida State's Bobby Bowden was going for his 319th victory Saturday night against Virginia.

Quotation—Paterno said: "The thing that's special for me is I've been able to coach that long. Not many guys get to coach 300 games. I've coached a lot and I've enjoyed it."

The winning score came on a 4-yard pass from Mills to Eric McCoo.

Paterno said after the game that he had not even thought about the record until asked about it. Deflecting the credit and focus to his players is a Paterno characteristic.

Penn State never led in the game until Robbie Gould kicked a 24-yard field goal with 3:36 left to put the Nittany Lions up by 31–28.

Northwestern quickly marched down the field behind quarterback Zak Kustok. He ran for his third touchdown of the game with 2:03 left to put the Wildcats on top, 35–31.

Mills was brilliant during his brief time on the field. He completed 5 of 8 passes during the drive, including the game winner to McCoo. The touchdown pass came on first down.

Quotation: Paterno said: "I thought it was great the way Zack went in cold. He's a very cool and poised kid."

Senneca had played well before being knocked out of the game. He had career-best totals of 20-of-39 passing for 234 yards, threw a 16-yard touchdown to McCoo and had the first two rushing touchdowns of his career, each from 1-yard out.

Kustok, the Big Ten leader in total offense, also had a great day. He was 23 of 40 passing for 298 yards and a touchdown to Sam Simmons. Kustok also rushed 21 times for 115 yards. Simmons had a big day receiving, grabbing seven passes for 168 yards.

3 Write a game story based on the following information, which is from an *Omaha* (Neb.) *World-Herald* story.

Dateline—Miami

The Nebraska Cornhuskers beat the Miami Hurricanes 24–17 in the FedEx Orange Bowl on Monday.

Nebraska finished the season 13–0 and likely will be named national champions when the final polls are released Tuesday.

The Cornhuskers were ranked No. 1 going into the game, but they had lost seven consecutive bowl games and were playing Miami, ranked No. 3, on its home field.

Nebraska's head coach, Tom Osborne, has been at the helm of the team for 22 years. This would be his first national championship.

Osborne, the nation's winningest active head coach, had been criticized for never winning a national championship, but he had always stressed that it is the journey each season that excites him, not merely the destination or outcome.

Known for showing little emotion on the sidelines, Osborne barely smiled as the clock wound down in the contest that was attended by an Orange-Bowl record crowd of 81,753. The crowd included an estimated 20,000 dressed in Cornhusker red.

The Cornhuskers entered the fourth quarter trailing 17–9. Nebraska marched 40 yards in two plays for a tying touchdown and 2-point conversion with 7:38 to play and then moved 59 yards in seven plays for the winning touchdown with 2:46 left.

Fullback Cory Schlesinger scored both touchdowns; the first was from 15 yards out, the second from 14 yards out.

Miami had won 62 of its past 63 home games over 10 years.

Nebraska roverback Kareem Moss intercepted Miami quarterback Frank Costa's desperation pass with 1:01 to play, thus sealing the NU victory.

Nebraska's defense was strong in the fourth quarter. The defense, nicknamed the Blackshirts, held the Hurricanes to minus 35 yards in the fourth quarter to build a final total yardage advantage of 305–277.

Cornhusker quarterback Tommie Frazier was named the most valuable player. He had come back from a 98-day layoff from injury and his execution of the Cornhuskers' option attack proved to be the difference.

Direct quotation from Frazier about Coach Osborne: "He's the type of person who doesn't show his feelings. But I guarantee you that once it sinks in for him, you'll see a couple of tears and a smile."

Frazier started the game, gave way to backup quarterback Brook Berringer (who had led the Cornhuskers to seven straight victories during the time Frazier was sidelined with his injury) for the middle two quarters and then entered the game in the fourth quarter to lead two touchdown drives in the final eight minutes.

Direct quotation from fullback Schlesinger: "This feels so good. This is what we have been working for all year, and it happened."

Schlesinger played eight-man football in tiny Duncan, Neb., before enrolling at NU.

Direct quotation from NU offensive tackle Rob Zatechka: "The defense really squared up at the end. They proved they are one of the best defenses in the country by stopping Miami when it counted."

Here is the scoring summary and final statistics, as published in the *World-Herald:*

FIRST QUARTER

NU-MIAMI

0–3 Miami field goal: 44 yards by Dane Prewitt. **Drive:** 31 yards in 10 plays. **Time elapsed:** 5:35. **Key plays:** Frank Costa passes of 10 yards to A.C. Tellison on third-and-five to NU 43 and 18 yards to Chris T. Jones on third-and-five to NU 20. Time left: 7:54.

0–10 Miami touchdown: Trent Jones 35-yard pass from Costa. **Conversion:** Prewitt kick. **Drive:** 97 yards in five plays. **Time elapsed:** 2:35. **Key play:** Tellison 43-yard pass from Costa. **Time left:** 0:04.

SECOND QUARTER

7–10 NU touchdown: Mark Gilman 19-yard pass from Brook Berringer. **Conversion:** Tom Sieler kick. **Drive:** 40 yards in five plays. **Time elapsed:** 2:20. **Key plays:** Lawrence Phillips 7-yard run to Miami 29;

Riley Washington 9 yards on reverse to Miami 20. **Time left:** 7:54.

THIRD QUARTER

7–17 Miami touchdown: Jonathan Harris 44-yard pass from Costa. **Conversion:** Prewitt kick. **Drive:** 78 yards in five plays. **Time elapsed:** 1:41. **Key play:** James Stewart 14-yard run to NU 45. **Time left:** 13:19.

9–17 NU safety: Dwayne Harris sacks Costa in end zone. **Time left:** 11:35.

FOURTH QUARTER

17–17 NU touchdown: Cory Schlesinger 15-yard run. **Conversion:** Eric Alford pass from Tommie Frazier. **Drive:** 40 yards in two plays. **Time elapsed:** :33. **Key play:** Phillips 25-yard run to Miami 15. **Time left:** 7:38.

24–17 NU touchdown: Schlesinger 14-yard run. **Conversion:** Sieler kick. **Drive:** 58 yards in seven plays. **Time elapsed:** 2:42. **Key plays:** Frazier 25-yard run on third-and-four to Miami 27; Frazier 6-yard run on third-and-3 to Miami 14. **Time left:** 2:46.

Score by Quarters

Miami	10	0	7	0—17
Nebraska	0	7	2	15—24

Category	NU	Miami
First downs	20	14
By rushing	15	4
By passing	4	10
By penalty	1	0
Rushes–yards	46–199	28–29
Avg. per carry	4.3	1.0
Comp.–att.–int.	11–20–2	18–35–1
Passing yards	106	248
Total yards	305	277
Total plays	66	63
Avg. per play	4.6	4.4
Punt returns–yards	4–17	2–(-6)
Kickoff returns–yards	5–88	2–40
Interceptions–yards	1–0	2–0
Fumbles–lost	2–1	2–0
Penalties–yards	3–20	11–92
Punts–average	7–41.1	7–39.7
Sacks by–yards lost	5–24	3–20
Third-down conversions	3–11	3–13
Time of possession	32:32	27:28

Attendance–81,753

4 Write a game story based on the following information, which is from an Associated Press story.

Dateline—Tempe, Ariz.

The Oregon Ducks beat the Colorado Buffaloes 38–16 in the Fiesta Bowl Tuesday. Oregon entered the game ranked No. 2; Colorado entered the game ranked No. 3.

Colorado scored first to take a 7–0 lead, but Oregon then reeled off 38 consecutive points. Oregon finished the season 11–1; Colorado finished 10–3.

The game had national championship implications.

Nebraska was scheduled to play No. 1 Miami two days later in the Rose Bowl. An upset by No. 4 Nebraska possibly would open the door for the winner of the Colorado-Oregon game to claim a split of the national championship.

Oregon quarterback Joey Harrington was impressive, closing his college career in grand fashion. He threw for 350 yards and four touchdowns.

Quotation: Harrington said: "We made a statement today. Thirty-eight unanswered points and shut down the hottest team in the country. We showed we deserved to be playing for a share of the national championship."

Samie Parker starred as a receiver. He caught nine passes for 162 yards. He caught a 79-yard touchdown pass from Harrington that put Oregon ahead for good in the second quarter. The second quarter was big for the Ducks; they outgained Colorado 198 yards to 53.

Oregon's defense, ranked 81st in the NCAA Division I entering the game, was suspect. But it shut down Colorado's running game and forced the Big 12 champions to throw. Oregon's Steve Smith led the defense; he made three interceptions, which set a Fiesta Bowl record.

Another great Oregon play in the second quarter came when Maurice Morris ran 49 yards to put his team up 28–7. He was hit and landed on top of a Colorado defender at the Buff 21-yard line, but he managed to get back on his feet without touching the ground and ran into the end zone.

Oregon's offense dominated, enjoying a 500–328 advantage in total yards. Oregon outrushed the Buffaloes 150–49.

Obviously, the Pacific 10 champions will be rooting for Nebraska.

Quotation: Quarterback Harrington: "You bet I will. I'll be sitting with my family and watching it closer than anyone else."

The best Oregon could hope for would be a split of the national championship. It could be voted the national champion in The Associated Press media poll. But the coaches'' poll automatically crowns the winner of the Bowl Championship Series game, which would be either Miami or Nebraska.

Harrington has had big games before at Sun Devil Stadium in Tempe. As a junior, he threw for career highs of 434 yards and six touchdowns during a 56–55 double-overtime win over Arizona State in a Pac-10 Conference game.

Harrington had a great college career. He finished 25–3 as a starter.

He was brilliant in the first half against Colorado, throwing for 232 yards and three touchdowns.

Colorado entered the game hot. It had trounced Nebraska 62–36 and had beaten Texas 39–37 in the Big 12 title game. It was the worst bowl loss ever for Colorado.

Colorado simply could not contain the Ducks. Oregon never had a touchdown drive longer than 2 minutes, 38 seconds.

Colorado quarterback Bobby Pesavento completed just 11 of 27 passes for 139 yards and was intercepted twice before he was relieved by Craig Ochs with 11:52 left in the game.

Ochs didn't get off to a good start. His first pass was deflected and intercepted by Smith. The interception set up Oregon's final touchdown.

Quotation: Oregon coach Mike Bellotti called the victory "the greatest moment in Duck football history."

Oregon won 11 games for the first time in its history.

Quotation: Colorado coach Gary Barnett, who said Oregon deserved a share of the national championship if Nebraska were to beat Miami: "Oregon played very, very well, with a lot of heart and a lot of speed. If I could vote, I would vote for them."

Here is the scoring summary and final statistics:

Fiesta Bowl

Oregon 38

Colorado 16

Colorado	7	0	0	9 —	16
Oregon	7	14	7	10 —	38

First Quarter

Col—Drumm 1 run (Brougham kick), 6:26.

Ore—Howry 28 pass from Harrington (Siegel kick), 3:48.

Second Quarter

Ore—Parker 79 pass from Harrington (Siegel kick), 3:13.

Ore—O.Smith 6 pass from Harrington (Siegel kick), 2:29.

Third Quarter

Ore—Morris 49 run (Siegel kick), 12:33.

Fourth Quarter

Ore—FG Siegel 47, 12:03.

Ore—Peelle 4 pass from Harrington (Siegel kick), 9:38.

Col—FG Flores 39, 5:47.

Col—Graham 4 pass from Ochs (kick failed), :18.

A—74,118.

	Col	Ore
First downs	20	22
Rushes-yards	31-49	28-150
Passes	279	350
Punt Returns	3-25	3-4
Kickoff Returns	7-159	3-49
Interceptions Ret.	1-14	3-35
Comp-Att-Int	24-47-3	28-42-1
Sacked-Yards Lost	4-25	0-0
Punts	5-40.8	5-36.2
Fumbles-Lost	1-0	0-0
Penalties-Yards	8-55	8-74
Time of Possession	28:55	31:05

INDIVIDUAL STATISTICS

RUSHING—Colorado Brown 9-30, Johnson 8-24, Purify 6-19, Drumm 1-1, Pesavento 2-(minus 5), Ochs 5-(minus 20). Oregon, Morris 11-89, O.Smith 14-51, Line 2-7, Willis 1-3.

PASSING—Colorado, Pesavento 11-27-2-139, Ochs 13-20-1-140. Oregon, Harrington 28-42-1-350.

REVEIVING—Colorado, Graham 10-89, McCoy 5-66, Johnson 3-50, Brunson 3-35, Cormier 2-25, Houston 1-14. Oregon, Parker 9-162, Willis 6-62, Peelle 5-66, Howry 3-33, O.Smith 3-8, Line 1-16, Wrighster 1-3.

MISSED FIELD GOAL—Colorado, Flores 47 (WL).

5 Write a game story based on the following information, which is from an Associated Press story.

Dateline—Pasadena, Calif.

Ninth-ranked Wisconsin and sixth ranked UCLA both took 10–1 records into the Rose Bowl.

Wisconsin was pleased to be in the game. UCLA, however, was disappointed because it had lost its last regular season game to Miami, 49–45, on Dec. 5. Had UCLA won that game, it would have played for the national championship in the Fiesta Bowl. Ironically, Kansas State, which also lost its last game before the bowl season (to Texas A&M) and which might have been invited to the Fiesta Bowl had it won, also was defeated in its bowl game: to Purdue in the Alamo Bowl.

Wisconsin beat UCLA 38–31 in the Rose Bowl that was played on Saturday.

Even though UCLA plays its home games in the Rose Bowl, it was Wisconsin who felt at home. Indeed, Wisconsin fans outnumbered Bruin fans about 2–1.

Ron Dayne led the Wisconsin offense with 246 yards rushing and a Rose Bowl record-tying four touchdowns.

The game saw 1,035 yards of offense from both teams. UCLA was led by quarterback Cade McNown, who passed for 340 yards and two touchdowns in his final game for the Bruins. However, he threw an interception that allowed the Badgers to open a 10-point lead early in the fourth quarter. Cornerback Jamar Fletcher intercepted McNown's pass—which was thrown straight to him. Fletcher returned the interception 47 yards to give the Badgers a 38–28 lead.

The Bruins tried to come back. Chris Sailer kicked a 30-yard field goal with 6:05 left in the game, but Wisconsin's defense shut down UCLA the rest of the way.

The Badgers, who until 1994 hadn't been to the Rose Bowl in 31 years and had never won the game, actually made it two victories in five years—both over UCLA.

Dayne, a 253-pound tailback, finished one yard short of Charles White's Rose Bowl rushing yardage record. Ironically, Wisconsin quarterback Mike Samuel dropped to one knee three times to run out the clock at the end of the game. Wisconsin coach Barry Alvarez said he wasn't aware that Dayne needed just one yard for the record.

Dayne ran with power through the middle of the line and he ran with speed in the open field. He carried the ball 27 times. His touchdowns came on runs of 54, 7, 10 and 22 yards.

This was the first year in the history of Wisconsin football that the Badgers won 11 games.

Direct quotation from Alvarez, who said he was happy that his team earned a spot in the Rose Bowl and even happier that it won: "It was a great football game; two teams playing very hard and a lot of guys making plays. We feel very fortunate to walk out of here with a win."

Direct quotation from UCLA coach Bob Toledo, who called the contest a "classic game": "They didn't do anything we didn't expect. It was an excellent, hard-fought game."

The Badgers pounded away all days on the porous UCLA defense, which was not able to stop Miami in the regular season finale either.

Direct quotation from quarterback McNown: "These last couple of games have been disappointing."

Direct quotation from Bruin flanker Freddie Mitchell: "Our defense was ready to redeem itself after the Miami game. They (the defenders) were really pumped up, but Wisconsin was just a better team than us."

Wisconsin savored the victory. Badger fans lingered for more than a half hour after the game, singing "On Wisconsin" and cheering as the band played and players danced on the field.

Part Six

Advanced Assignments

23

In-Depth and Investigative Reporting

Review Questions

1 What is an in-depth?

2 Why is it a misconception that investigative reporting started during the Watergate era of the 1970s?

3 In-depths are choice assignments, yet they are also grueling. Explain why.

4 Why do reporters, particularly investigative reporters, continually follow hunches?

5 The chapter lists five reasons why careful research is vital to an in-depth article. List and discuss them.

a

b

c

d

e

6 Why is it important to understand and use public records when working on an in-depth or investigative story?

7 In some in-depths, the interviews are done "from the outside in." What does that mean?

8 What is a smoking-gun interview, and why are some reporters opposed to it?

9 Why is it so important for in-depth and investigative reporters to double- and triple-check everything their sources tell them?

10 What are the four general guidelines that reporters follow in dealing with confidential sources?

a

b

c

d

11 Discuss the pros and cons of undercover journalism.

12 William Recktenwald, a former *Chicago Tribune* reporter who was involved in numerous undercover investigations, says that reporters should avoid going undercover unless it is absolutely necessary. What advice does he give to reporters involved in undercover work?

13 Why is a strong thread so important in an in-depth article?

14 Discuss the advantages of a first-person article.

Suggested Exercises

Your assignment is to write an in-depth article. Follow these steps:

1 Produce a story idea for the in-depth. It should include:

  a Purpose of the story

  b Why the story is necessary

  c Possible sources

2 Conduct library and/or online research, and make appointments for interviews.

3 After the interviewing is over, outline the story and discuss it with your instructor.

4 Write a suggested lead for the story, and discuss it with your instructor. If you write a lead block, also write the nut graph. Explain why you think your lead is the best. Rewrite if necessary.

5 Write the story. Make certain that it has a thread holding together the beginning, middle and end.

24

Business News and Other Specialties

Review Questions

1 Discuss the differences between specialty reporters and beat reporters and the increasing role of business writers in today's media.

2 What advice does business reporter Mary Beth Sammons give to aspiring business writers?

3 Define the following terms.

a Publicly held company

b Privately held company

c Annual report

d Auditor's report

e Assets

f Current assets

g Liabilities

h Current liabilities

i Shareowners' equity

j Sales

k Net income

l Quarterly report

4 What are some buzzwords that reporters can look for in an auditor's report or in a letter from the chairperson to spot potential trouble within a company?

5 Consumer reporting has come far since its emergence in the 1960s and early 1970s, but it still has a long way to go. Discuss consumer reporting in print and broadcast today, and compare that with consumer reporting in 1965, when consumer advocate Ralph Nader published "Unsafe at Any Speed: The Designed-In Dangers of the American Automobile."

6 What tips do Dan Gillmor of the *San Jose Mecury News* and syndicated columnist Kim Komando give about technology reporting?

7 What tips do Casey Bukro of the *Chicago Tribune* and John G. Mitchell of *National Geographic* magazine give for becoming an environmental writer?

Suggested Exercises

1 Examine the dominant metropolitan newspaper in your area for several days. What subject areas are covered by specialty reporters? What specialty areas are not being covered?

2 Clip from a daily newspaper a story on a specialized subject. What steps did the reporter probably follow in writing the story? Who was interviewed? Are there holes in the story? Is it written in inverted-pyramid style with a summary lead or is it a feature?

3 To localize national "Small Business Is Big in the USA Week," financial writer Mary Beth Sammons wrote a profile for *The Daily Herald* in Arlington Heights, Ill., of two small-business people who had been honored for their success by local chambers of commerce. Following are the notes she compiled for one of the profiles. Write a story using her notes as though they were your own.

From the Illinois Department of Commerce and Community Affairs: There are 225,000 businesses with fewer than 500 employees in the state. They account for 94.4% of Illinois business.

Interview with Peter Lineal: Owner of Plum Grove Printers in Schaumburg and recent recipient of the Northwest Suburban Association of Commerce and Industry's "Small Business Person of the Year" award.

He's 31. He founded the one-man

printing shop at age 26 after following a traditional path after college graduation, landing a job in his major at a small advertising and publishing firm. Although promotions soon followed, he became frustrated after five years and decided to pursue his own business venture.

Because opening a business would be such a financial burden on his family, Lineal also assumed the daily care of his infant while his wife worked full time to pay the bills during the first year of the print shop's operation.

Funny story about meeting clients with an infant strapped to his stomach in a Snugli: "It seems hard to believe when I look back on it, but I used to carry the baby strapped in a Snugli to my chest while I ran the presses and took customer orders. One day, when I was in the middle of a sales pitch to these three women, the baby woke up and was just screaming. There I was trying to calm the baby and win over some customers. It was quite a comical sight." The clients were from the Concrete Reinforced Steel Institute in Schaumburg. Today it is one of Plum Grove Printers' biggest accounts.

Staff of 13 full-time and part-time employees now. Company's profits have risen sharply after a profit of $172 the first year.

Business philosophy: "I tell my salespersons and my entire staff that they work for the customer, not for me. If the customer says don't worry about some detail, I insist that we worry about it anyway. We've always got to take that extra step. If you take care of the customer, he takes care of you."

On that terrible first year: "The first year we were in business was pretty grim because we were in a storefront that wasn't visible from the road. I think many small business persons make similar mistakes like that and it can be quite costly."

He says "profitability" is what it takes to be successful. "You've got to control costs, and by that I mean count all the pennies and nickels. When you start making a profit, you have a real tendency to grow, grow, grow, but you've got to have a cost-controlled and carefully calculated growth."

4 Write a consumer-oriented story based on the following information, which is from an Associated Press story. The story is datelined Washington. (Note: The original story used a direct-address lead and direct address throughout.)

This story is about the U.S. tax system. It deals with the earned-income credit.

The earned-income credit offers a bonus of up to $910 a year to low-income working families with children.

The maximum credit of $910 is available only to families with income between $6,500 and $10,250, but some benefit can be claimed until income reaches $19,340.

A qualifying worker can receive the benefit in advance as part of his or her weekly paycheck.

Workers may qualify if they meet all of these tests:

- Had at least one child who lived with applying worker more than half of the year, or for the entire year if the worker files as a qualifying widow or widower.
- Had earned income—wages, tips or self-employment earnings—of less than $19,340 last year.
- Had adjusted gross income—total income subject to tax minus alimony, employee business expenses and similar adjustments—under $19,340.
- File a joint return, as head of household or qualifying widow or widower with dependent child.

There are different rules applying to each of the three filing statuses. IRS Publication 596, which is free, has details.

You may calculate the credit yourself by using the special work sheet and the earned-income-credit table in your tax instructions. Or the IRS will figure the credit for you. The instructions are on page 31 of the 1040A instructions or page 16 of the 1040 booklet.

5 Outline a story in a specialized area that you would like to cover. Why is the story necessary? Is it a news story or a feature? What type of library research or online research would you do? Who would you interview?

6 Now it is time to write the story. You are probably not a specialist yet, and so you should take your time. Make certain that you have researched the story well and have learned some of the language of the specialized area before you begin the interviewing process.

Part Seven

Beyond the Writing

25

Law

Review Questions

1 Some people contend that the First Amendment provides absolute protection for journalists. Discuss.

2 Define and discuss the following:

a Libel

b "Cyberlibel"

c Journalists' privilege

d Fair trial versus free press

3 List five requirements that must be met before a libel action can be brought successfully.

a

b

c

d

e

4 The chapter discusses four categories of words that are considered libelous in the state of Illinois. Classes of libelous words can, of course, vary slightly among the states, but the Illinois list is representative. List the classes of words discussed.

a Category 1

b Category 2

c Category 3

d Category 4

5 List and discuss conditional defenses against libel.

6 List and discuss absolute defenses against libel.

7 List and discuss partial defenses against libel.

8 Discuss the "actual malice" standard articulated in *New York Times Co.* v. *Sullivan.*

9 Why is the status of the plaintiff—public or private—one of the most important considerations in a libel case?

10 Discuss the impact of *Gertz* v. *Robert Welch* on libel law.

11 Discuss the impact of the *Sharon* libel case.

12 Discuss how the threat of libel actions can be economically intimidating.

13 The New York State Newspapers Foundation, in its "Survival Kit for Reporters, Editors and Broadcasters," provides advice for potential libel defendants. List the tips.

14 What are shield laws? Discuss the level of protection they provide journalists.

15 Journalists often claim that they do not have to reveal confidential information or the names of anonymous sources when called on to do so in a court of law. Discuss whether such a protection flows from the common law, the statutory law or the First Amendment.

16 List and discuss some procedural safeguards that judges should consider to help ensure that the accused receives a fair trial, while allowing the press its rights to report freely.

17 Are cameras allowed in federal courtrooms? In state courtrooms?

18 Do journalists enjoy special First Amendment protection when it comes to *gathering* information?

19 Do student journalists enjoy the same legal protections that apply to journalists at professional media outlets?

Suggested Exercises

1 Assume that you have just written an article critical of a state senator in your area. You misinterpreted the facts on which you based the story. There is no doubt; the story is not accurate. You made a mistake—but it was not intentional. The story contains a defamatory falsehood. This is extremely unfortunate because the state senator is your personal friend. You are embarrassed, and he is irritated. Friendship

aside, he sues you and your newspaper for libel. What would be possible defenses? Would you have a good chance of successfully defending against the libel action?

2 Assume that your newspaper is sued for $50,000 in general damages and $50,000 in punitive damages by John Jones, M.D., who claimed that the newspaper had published an article stating that he is the only physician at General Hospital who has been successfully sued for malpractice during the past two years. In fact, however, Dr. Jones is the only physician at General Hospital who has *not* been sued successfully for malpractice during the past two years. Dr. Jones, in the complaint he filed, said that he has a sound reputation as a medical doctor, as evidenced by having been honored by the American Medical Association the previous year for outstanding contributions to the local medical association. He claimed that the wholly false statement is libelous and caused him to suffer "deep pain, anguish and humiliation." The evidence indicates that the newspaper, in preparing the story, inadvertently misinterpreted the correct facts, which were spelled out clearly in court records. Does the doctor have a good case? Discuss in terms of the various common law or statutory defenses. Then discuss in terms of the defenses available as a result of *Sullivan* and other relevant decisions.

3 As you read the discussion of *Gertz* v. *Robert Welch* in this chapter, you should have noticed that the decision left it up to the individual states to define appropriate levels of fault—negligence—when libel suits are brought by private persons involved in events of general or public interest. Nearly all of the states have since defined negligence. Is your state one of them? What is the standard?

4 Assume that you have just finished a story that deals with the illegal operation of unlicensed abortion agencies in your community. You have spent considerable time at the agencies. Now you must consider the possible legal ramifications of the story—particularly because you have learned that a local grand jury is investigating this very issue. In the event that the grand jury calls you to testify, what options would be available to you if you do not want to reveal confidential information?

5 Assume that you are attending a meeting of your state's press association. One of the editors attending the meeting tells you that he is disturbed by the increasing number of gag orders being placed on the press in various trials. He says he feels that the First Amendment precludes any type of interference from the judiciary and that procedural safeguards are available to the accused. The editor says that the press is responsible in covering litigation and that judges should keep their hands off the media. In order for him to understand some of the blatant abuses by the press when covering litigation, you point out the circumstances in *Irvin* v. *Dowd, Rideau* v. *Louisiana* and *Sheppard* v. *Maxwell.* What would you tell the editor?

6 Assume that a murder trial is being conducted in your community. You are assigned to cover it. The judge announces, however, that he is barring the press from the preliminary hearing, but he is allowing the public to attend. What might you tell the judge?

7 Locate and read in your school's library or law library a significant Supreme Court decision that has a profound effect on you as a working journalist. For example, you might read *New York Times Co.* v. *Sullivan,* 376 U.S. 254 (1964), or *Gertz* v. *Robert Welch,* 418 U.S. 323 (1974), two important libel decisions. Write a news story that summarizes the important segments of the decision you have chosen.

26

Ethics and Fairness: Responsibility to Society

Review Questions

1 Why have journalists increasingly found themselves on the hot seat of public opinion?

2 As the 21st century approached, The Freedom Forum, a nonpartisan, international foundation dedicated to free press, free speech and free spirit for all people, embarked on a multimillion-dollar project to study and make recommendations for improving fairness in journalism. What was the *premise* of that project?

3 Robert H. Giles, longtime metropolitan daily newspaper editor and publisher and director of The Freedom Forum's Free Press/Fair Press project, outlined five concerns raised by the public that go to the heart of the journalistic process. List and discuss the five concerns.

a

b

c

d

e

4 Charles L. Overby, Freedom Forum chairman and chief executive officer, has broken down the components of fairness into five basic categories that provide an easy-to-read formula: a+b+c+d+e=f. List and discuss.

a

b

c

d

e

f

5 List and discuss the nine examples of unfairness in newspapers that are featured in Robert Haiman's Best Practices for Newspaper Journalists.

a

b

c

d

e

f

g

h

i

6 List and discuss the "good questions to make good ethical decisions" compiled by Bob Steele, director, Ethics Program, Poynter Institute for Media Studies.

a

b

c

d

e

f

g

h

i

j

7 Discuss the following.

a Authoritarian press system

b Libertarian press system

c Social responsibility theory

8 What is the function of a media critic?

9 What is the function of an ombudsman?

10 Under the heading "The Ethics of Journalism," the chapter quotes from one of John Merrill's books, "The Imperative of Freedom." In that excerpt, Professor Merrill distinguishes between ethics and law. Discuss the distinction.

11 The textbook cites two surveys of random samples of the country's daily newspaper managing editors. The surveys showed that eight primary issues emerged when respondents were asked to list and discuss what they considered to be the most pressing ethical issues facing journalists today. The eight issues are listed below. Provide an overview of each issue, based on the discussion presented in the textbook and on your opinions.

a Fairness and objectivity

b Misrepresentation by reporters

c Economic pressure

d Privacy versus the public's right to know

e Conflicts of interest

f Anonymous sources

g Gifts

h Compassion versus policy

Suggested Exercises

1 At a meeting of the Organization of News Ombudsmen, it was noted that many newspapers send out questionnaires to news subjects, asking them if they found the stories about themselves to be fair and accurate. These surveys, which *Editor & Publisher* magazine said can be traced to 1945 when the *Minneapolis Star* and *Tribune* instituted the practice, are used to bridge the credibility gap between news media and their audiences. Discuss whether you think these surveys are worth the effort to conduct them.

2 A reporter works in one of the states that does not have a law prohibiting the taping of a telephone conversation without telling the other party. The reporter is working on an investigative story about possible price-fixing among major contractors that have been awarded contracts from the state. The reporter wants to make sure that he accurately reports what his sources tell him during telephone interviews. He decides to tape-record the interviews. Because there is no law in his state that mandates informing the other party, the reporter decides that it is not necessary to do so. Do you agree?

3 A reporter works for a 20,000-circulation daily. She earns $400 per week. Her job is to cover city government. Her most visible assignment is coverage of the city council. The manager of a local theater is not an elected city official, but he is very active in civic affairs. He often attends city council meetings. He introduces himself to the reporter one evening and tells the reporter that he is impressed with her fair, balanced, accurate coverage of council meetings. He gives the reporter a complimentary pass to see all movies at the theater during the next calendar year. What would you do if you were given a complimentary movie pass under these circumstances?

4 The sports editor of a 50,000-circulation morning newspaper has been covering athletics at the local college for more than 20 years. Five times, he has been named the state's sportswriter of the year. The sports editor has never been accused of being a cheerleader for local teams, nor has he ever been accused of being critical and cynical merely for the sake of showing coaches and athletes that he is in control. Balanced, accurate, descriptive writing is his trademark. The sports editor has a 16-year-old son who is an exceptional basketball player. Each summer, the local college coach holds a one-week basketball camp for players in the area. Players pay $200 to participate. The coach tells the sports editor that, because his son has been such an avid fan of the local college team, he is going to let the boy attend the camp free of charge. If you were the sports editor, how would you respond?

5 Millions of readers across the country look forward to opening their Sunday newspapers to the travel section. The reading can provide a pleasant escape from reality. A Midwestern housewife who cannot get her car out of the driveway because of snowdrifts can read about cruises to exotic Pacific islands. An urban apartment dweller can read about a spacious luxury hotel in the south of France. Many of these stories are written by the travel editors of the newspapers. Some of these journalists gather information for their stories while on trips paid for by the hotels they visit or by the cruise lines whose ships they sail on. Does this pose ethical problems?

6 A reporter for a 15,000-circulation afternoon daily covers city and county government. Each day, she dutifully makes her rounds: the police department, the county sheriff's office, the clerk of the court, the city engineer's office, the city clerk's office and so forth. During the Christmas holidays, three of her regular sources give her gifts: a small box of chocolates, a novel and an inexpensive pen and pencil set. Should she accept the gifts?

7 The wife of the education reporter for a 25,000-circulation daily in a community of 40,000 decides to run for city council. The education reporter is not involved in coverage of city government issues or in coverage of the city council. The managing editor calls the reporter into his office. The managing editor tells the reporter that he has two choices: persuade his wife to drop out of the political race or resign his job because of a potential conflict of interest. Do you agree with the managing editor?

8 The city beat reporter for a 15,000-circulation daily is responsible for gathering information from county court. The newspaper's policy is to print the names of all persons charged with driving while intoxicated. The reporter regularly attends services at a local church. His minister approaches him one Sunday morning after services. The minister says that a parishioner who has significant personal problems was arrested Saturday night for driving while intoxicated. He will be charged in county court on Monday. The minister says that he is aware of the newspaper's policy about printing the names of those charged. The minister says that he hates to put any pressure on the reporter. The minister says, however, that he is convinced that the person will ultimately be found innocent of the charge. The minister notes that this is the first time he has ever asked a favor of the reporter, but he is very

worried about the sick, elderly aunt of the parishioner who has been charged. The minister says he thinks if the woman reads about the arrest in the newspaper, it could be mentally and physically devastating for her. The minister suggests that the reporter not print the story about the charges being filed. Later, if the person is found guilty, the story could be published at that time. The reporter has great respect and admiration for the minister, a man to whom he once went for counseling when he was deeply troubled by a personal problem. The reporter agrees to the request. Under the circumstances, do you think the reporter made the right decision?

9 David Shaw, national press reporter for the *Los Angeles Times,* wrote that "the arrogance of the press may be one of the greatest problems we, as an institution, face today." React to Shaw's statement.

10 Sandra Mims Rowe, editor of *The Oregonian* in Portland and former president of the American Society of Newspaper Editors, told the nation's ombudsmen: "Credibility is not theoretical, philosophical or remote from our work. It is at the heart of our professional lives. Credibility is not about selling more newspapers. It is about building the quality and integrity of our news. It is not about finding some new journalistic fad or silver bullet to solve our problems. It is about thoroughly understanding, clearly articulating and relentlessly applying the highest professional and ethical standards." React to her statement.

Permissions and Credits

Chapter 3

Pages 18–20 (exercise 3): Reprinted with permission of *The Hartford* (Conn.) *Courant.*

Chapter 4

Page 32 (exercise 26): Used with permission of *The East Valley Tribune.*

Chapter 5

Page 35 (exercise 1): *Chicago Tribune.* Pages 36–37 (exercise 3): *Iowa State Daily.* Page 39 (exercise 9): Copyright © 1986, *Indiana Daily Student;* reprinted with permission. Pages 39–40 (exercise 11): *Daily Forty-Niner,* California State University, Long Beach. Page 40 (exercise 12): The Associated Press; used by permission of The Associated Press.

Chapter 6

Pages 42–43 (exercise 1): The Associated Press; used by permission of The Associated Press. Page 43 (exercise 2): The Associated Press; used by permission of The Associated Press. Pages 45–46 (exercise 5): The Associated Press; used by permission of The Associated Press.

Chapter 9

Page 61 (exercise 1): Used with permission of the *The East Valley Tribune.* Pages 62–63 (exercise 3): The Associated Press; used by permission of The Associated Press.

Chapter 10

Pages 70–72 (exercise 1): Denise Franklin, *Santa Cruz* (Calif.) *Sentinel.*

Chapter 12

Pages 85–89 (exercises 1, 2, 3, 4, 5, 6): Used or reprinted with permission of the University News Bureau, University of North Carolina.

Chapter 13

Page 96 (exercise 2): *The Evansville* (Ind.) *Press.* Pages 97–102 (exercises 5, 6, 7, 8, 9, 10, 11): The Associated Press; used by permission of The Associated Press.

Chapter 16

Pages 127–128 (exercises 2, 3): Reprinted with permission of the *Hastings* (Neb.) *Tribune.* Pages 128–129 (exercise 4): The Associated Press; used by permission of The Associated Press. Page 129 (exercise 5): Reprinted with permission of *The Arizona Republic.* Pages 129–130 (exercise 6): Reprinted with permission of *The Beaumont* (Texas) *Enterprise.* Page 130 (exercise 7): *The Gleaner,* Henderson, Ky. Pages 130–131 (exercise 8): The Associated Press; used by permission of The Associated Press.

Chapter 17

Pages 135–137 (exercises 2, 3, 4, 5, 6, 7): The Associated Press; used by permission of The Associated Press. Page 138 (exercises 8, 9): Used with permission of KOOL-FM, Phoenix, Ariz.

Chapter 18

Page 145 (exercise 3): © *San Francisco Chronicle;* Reprinted by permission.

Chapter 19

Pages 150–151 (exercise 1): Reprinted with permission of *The Birmingham* (Ala.) *News.* Page 151 (exercise 2): Reprinted with permission of the *Hastings* (Neb.) *Tribune.* Page 152 (exercise 3): Reprinted with permission of *The Birmingham* (Ala.) *News.* Page 153 (exercise 4): Used with permission of Star-Herald Publishing Company, Inc. Scottsbluff, Neb. Pages 153–154 (exercise 5): Used with permission of the *Colorado Springs* (Colo.) *Gazette Telegraph.* Pages 154–155 (exercise 6): Reprinted with permission of *The Beaumont* (Texas) *Enterprise.* Pages 155–157 (exercise 7): *The Gleaner,* Henderson, Ky.

Chapter 20

Page 162 (exercise 4): Used with permission of the *Colorado Springs* (Colo.) *Gazette Telegraph.* Pages 162–163 (exercise 5): *Fairbanks* (Alaska) *Daily News-Miner.*

Chapter 21

Pages 175–176 (exercise 6): Reprinted with permission of the *Plano* (Texas) *Star Courier.* Page 184 (exercise 9): The Associated Press; used by permission of The Associated Press.

Chapter 22

Page 197 (exercise 2): The Associated Press; used by permission of The Associated Press. Pages 198–199 (exercise 3): Reprinted with permission of the *Omaha* (Neb.) *World-Herald.* Pages 199–201 (exercises 4–5): The Associated Press; used by permission of The Associated Press.